Table of Contents

CHAPTER ONE

Smart Money Management

How to Protect Your Money from The People Who Protect the Places that Protect Your Money

Most of us who have accounts at banks or savings-and-loan institutions know little about Federal Deposit Insurance Corporation (FDIC) protection.

This lack of knowledge can be costly if your bank or savings-and-loan goes under—for part of your money may not be insured. Answers to the most common questions about FDIC coverage...

•*Are all banks and savings-and-loans protected by the FDIC?* Most banks are protected, but some private banks are not. Be sure to look for the FDIC label on your bank's door or at the tellers' windows.

•*Are all individual accounts covered separately by the FDIC? Up to how much?* Most people know that the FDIC covers individual accounts up to $100,000. What they don't know is that an individual account is determined by adding up each account held under a common name or Social Security number.

Example: If a person has a savings account with $50,000 in it and a Certificate of Deposit for $60,000 at the same bank, $10,000 is uninsured.

Accounts set up under the Uniform Gifts to Minors Act are considered to be the child's account, even though the parent has control over it.

•*What about joint accounts? Are they fully protected?* Joint accounts held by the same combination of persons at the same bank are only protected up to $100,000, regardless of whose Social Security number appears on them.

Example: A husband and wife with two joint accounts of $100,000 each are insured only up to $100,000, not $200,000.

Avoid this restriction by using both individual and joint accounts.

Example: If you have an individual savings account of $100,000 and a joint savings account with your spouse of $100,000 at the same bank, each account has full protection. Your spouse can have an individual savings account of $100,000 and receive full coverage on it as well.

•*Are all deposits covered by the FDIC?* Mutual funds and other investments made through a bank are not protected. If you have any questions concerning FDIC insurance, call the FDIC at 800-934-3342 or visit www.fdic.gov.

•*Are trust accounts treated separately by the FDIC?* Yes, but only if the trusts are for members of your immediate family—a spouse, child or grandchild. But, if you set up an account in trust for your father, for example, it is treated as part of your account.

Trust accounts for a spouse, child or grandchild (including step- and adopted children) enjoy separate coverage, even if you have both an individual and a joint account.

Example: If you have an individual account with $100,000, a joint account with your spouse of $100,000 and a trust account for your spouse of $100,000, the accounts are all fully insured.

•*Can an individual open accounts at several branches of the same bank and receive full protection for each?* You cannot increase the limit of coverage by depositing funds in different branches of the same bank.

Self-defense: Diversify your funds among several banks.

•*Are IRAs and self-employed retirement plans fully protected?* Retirement accounts are lumped together to determine coverage.

Example: If you have an IRA of $50,000 and a self-employed retirement plan of $65,000 at the same bank, $15,000 is uninsured.

Self-defense: As CDs in an IRA or self-employed retirement plan mature, roll over sufficient amounts to other institutions to maximize FDIC coverage.

Source: Cody Buck, a former senior executive of the FDIC's division of liquidation and author of *The ABCs of FDIC: How to Save Your Assets From Liquidation.* CoStarr Publications.

Printed in the United States of America

Safer than Banks

Investors suffering from high anxiety are turning more and more to the safest investment there is: US Treasury securities.

Treasury bills (maturing within one year), notes (maturing in two to 10 years) and bonds (maturing after 10 years) are actually safer than government-insured bank accounts. *Trap:* There's only pennies in government insurance for every dollar of insured bank accounts. *Even worse:* Some of the insurance funds aren't in cash, but in illiquid receivables accepted from troubled banks.

By contrast, every penny of a T-bill is guaranteed by the full faith and credit of the federal government. And the government has never failed to pay its obligations.

Bonus: Liquidity, especially if they're purchased through a mutual fund that offers check-writing privileges. *Special tax status:* T-bills, notes and bonds bought by individuals aren't subject to state income taxes. When these securities are purchased through a mutual fund, 25 states levy a tax.

Source: James M. Benham, chairman, Benham Capital Management Group, 755 Page Mill Rd., Palo Alto, CA 94304.

How to Protect Yourself From Banks' New Services

Banks are offering an avalanche of "new" services that are just old services—repackaged. And, they are charging you for them.

Charges for some bank services have gone up 400% since the banking industry's deregulation in the mid-1980s.

How Your Bank May Be Squeezing You...

•Controlled disbursement services—your ability to transfer money electronically to cover checks. This used to take only a call to your bank. Now many banks charge customers $1 or more for these off-site transactions.

•Overdraft service. In the good old days, you could call your bank and ask to be notified if a check came in that your funds couldn't cover. Then, they would give you a chance to deposit money that day to cover the check. Now, overdraft services cost consumers a hefty service fee—plus, if you have overdraft "protection," interest on the "borrowed" funds.

•Automatic Teller Machines (ATMs) used to be a free service—but now many banks charge 50 cents to $1.50 for each transaction.

•Calling in for balances—and a record of checks cashed. You once could call your friendly teller for this service, free of charge—but it now may be costly.

•Home-equity lines of credit are just repackaged second mortgages...with a bundle of additional service fees tacked on.

Self-Defense

When you shop for a bank—compare the fees on new services. Go with the bank that has the lowest fees for the services you use most ...and stay away from the routine use of ATMs.

Don't immediately opt for the checking and savings account packages that have a lot of services attached.

If you only write a few checks a month, ask the bank for its low-cost, minimum standard checking account. And if you're a student, or disabled or a senior citizen, ask for a service-charge–free checking account. Most banks make these available, although few promote this service.

Get to Know Your Banker

If you know your banker, go to the bank and ask him/her to phone you to let you know when an overdraft occurs—instead of paying for an overdraft "service." And, if you know your banker, you are much more likely to get a loan... be able to negotiate service charges, fees and loan interest rates...or get a dispute with the bank solved quickly and favorably.

You should know at least one teller, a loan officer and a vice president at your bank. These are the people that can solve virtually every banking problem you encounter. I call this preventive maintenance.

Source: Edward Mrkvicka, Jr., president, Reliance Enterprises Inc., 22115 O'Connell Rd., Marengo, IL 60152. He is author of several books, including *Your Bank Is Ripping You Off.* St. Martin's Press.

Don't Pay Too Much

Nearly three out of four mortgage holders pay too much into escrow accounts—set up by lenders with a borrower's money to pay real-estate taxes and home-insurance costs. *Self-defense:* Check monthly payments carefully against copies of all tax and insurance bills. If what's due in taxes is less than the funds in escrow—seek a refund immediately. *Bottom line:* While you pay monthly, the lender might pay only quarterly—or even annually. Any funds held in escrow until those payments come due are the equivalent of giving the lender a no- or low-interest loan.

Source: Edward Mrkvicka, Jr., president, Reliance Enterprises Inc., 22115 O'Connell Rd., Marengo, IL 60152. He is author of several books, including *Your Bank Is Ripping You Off.* St. Martin's Press.

Bank-Failure Loophole

If your bank fails and your deposits exceed $100,000 (the maximum amount insured by the FDIC), you may be able to use the uninsured portion to pay off any outstanding debt you may have to the bank. *Self-defense:* Request a "voluntary offset" from the bank's claims agent. *Example:* Someone with $120,000 in deposits and a $50,000 bank loan can ask that the $20,000 not covered by the FDIC be used to pay down the loan. *Rationale:* You probably won't see the $20,000 for some time, and when you do, you aren't likely to receive the full amount. Meanwhile, your debt would be reduced by the amount offset, dollar for dollar.

Source: Cody Buck, a former senior executive of the FDIC's division of liquidation and author of *The ABCs of FDIC: How to Save Your Assets from Liquidation.* CoStarr Publications.

Bank Safe-Deposit-Box Trap

In effect, many banks don't insure safe-deposit boxes for theft. If there is insurance, it is very difficult to collect because you can't prove the box's contents. You could have a bank officer sign a safekeeping receipt each time you visit to confirm the contents...but this sacrifices your confidentiality and doesn't guarantee coverage. *Best:* A home safe. Models that exceed the fire safety of a bank vault cost less than $250 and losses are covered by your homeowner's insurance. List each item in a policy rider.

Source: Edward Mrkvicka, Jr., president, Reliance Enterprises Inc., 22115 O'Connell Rd., Marengo, IL 60152. He is author of several books including *Your Bank Is Ripping You Off.* St. Martin's Press.

ATM Self-Defense

Use only the machines at your own bank's branches...look for warnings of surcharges on ATMs not owned by your bank...avoid ATMs operated by independent companies, which are often in nontraditional locations and generally charge high fees...use credit or debit cards or traveler's checks to pay for purchases while traveling—instead of using ATMs...make fewer withdrawals, for larger sums—surcharges aren't based on the amount withdrawn.

Source: Edward Mrkvicka, Jr., president, Reliance Enterprises Inc., 22115 O'Connell Rd., Marengo, IL 60152. He is author of several books including *Your Bank Is Ripping You Off.* St. Martin's Press.

Beware of Bank IRAs

Retirement planning: One cannot overstate the importance of it. And...in investigating all of your Individual Retirement Account (IRA) options, I believe you'll find that a bank IRA is one of the least acceptable alternatives.

In fact, a bank IRA could be the most unrewarding investment you ever make.

Some banks advertise how you can "easily" accumulate a million dollars in your IRA.

Unfortunately, a Government Accounting Office study revealed that if inflation continues at its historical pace, your million dollars may be worth, in buying power, only $50,000. In other words, you'll be lucky to get back exactly what you put in.

There are other investments that could return much more for your retirement—even if you have to pay taxes on them.

Problem: Banks like IRAs for one reason and one reason only—they are cheap money for the banks. Bank IRA interest rates are historically one to three percentage points below those of other market IRA vehicles available from brokers and mutual-fund families. In later years, when your IRA balance is substantial, that could mean tens of thousands of dollars in interest lost every year.

Bigger problem: The banks' below-market IRA interest rates can be even more unfavorable. Under some plans, the bank also maintains the right to change the basis on which it pays interest, at its own discretion.

The insurance trap: Too many older investors say to me, "Never mind that I may be sacrificing some interest—at least I know that my retirement funds are insured by the full faith and credit of the US government."

For many years investors could have confidence in government insurance, at least up to the maximum insured limit—currently $100,000 (IRA balances in excess of $100,000 are not insured). But in the past 10 years, everything has changed.

We should have learned from the savings-and-loan disaster about the questionable value of government-backed deposit insurance.

Sooner or later there will be failures of major money-center banks—banks that have been getting away with privatizing their profits and socializing their losses by claiming they're "too big to fail."

As with the savings-and-loan bailout, this means that US taxpayers—you and I—will pay for those bank losses caused by illegal behavior, greed, incompetent regulatory agencies and a Congress that looks the other way.

Don't invest in a bank IRA because of bank insurance that is coming right out of your pocket.

Source: Edward Mrkvicka, Jr., president, Reliance Enterprises Inc., 22115 O'Connell Rd., Marengo, IL 60152. He is author of several books, including *Your Bank Is Ripping You Off.* St. Martin's Press.

Taking Money Out of an IRA

Is it true that one can take money out of an IRA before age 59½ without paying the 10% premature-distribution penalty if payments are received in the form of a lifetime annuity?

Yes, and this opens tax-planning opportunities. *Example:* In one case, a person took early annuity payments from an IRA and used them to make mortgage payments on a new house. The mortgage-interest deduction sheltered the annuity payments from income tax. The undistributed funds that remained in the IRA continued to earn tax-deferred income that could be used to make future mortgage payments.

Thus, the individual had found a tax-favored way to finance his new home. In a private ruling, the IRS held that the arrangement was proper.

How to Save a Million Dollars On an Inherited IRA

A married couple must plan ahead so they'll know in advance how to handle an IRA that one spouse inherits from the other.

Vital: There are choices to make about the IRA. Make the wrong choice and the IRA dies with the surviving spouse. Make the right choice and the IRA can continue for decades, accumulating tax-deferred income. A modest sum can easily grow from a few hundred thousand to a million dollars or more.

Trap: Many otherwise well-informed taxpayers don't know even the basics of how to handle an inherited IRA.

The basics: A person who inherits an IRA from a spouse has the choice of treating it in one of two ways:

•Take the inherited account as a beneficiary.

•Treat the inherited fund as your own, and roll it over into a new account in your own name.

The choice made can have huge consequences if, as is usually the case, the deceased spouse was over age 70½ when he/she died. The law requires the IRA owner to begin taking distributions by April 1 following the year in which he attains age 70½. After required distributions have begun...

•When the spouse takes the inherited IRA as a beneficiary, distributions generally must be made over the surviving spouse's life expectancy.

•When a spouse takes the inherited IRA as his/her own, distributions can be made over the combined life expectancies of the spouse and a newly named beneficiary.

Key: Because the beneficiary may be much younger than the inheriting spouse—40 or 50 years younger in the case of a grandchild—a huge tax-deferral can result, producing an extra 40 or 50 years of compound tax-deferred income in the account before it is fully distributed.

Payoff: In the fairly common case where an inherited IRA contains a few hundred thousand dollars—which may represent a lifetime of retirement savings rolled over from a company pension plan—several extra decades of tax-deferred compound earnings can easily amount to a million dollars or more.

An example of how the rules work:

Say that a husband is 78 and his wife is 74 in 2001, and they have a nine-year-old grandchild. The husband and wife are required to make IRA withdrawals over their joint life expectancy, which is 19.2 years according to IRS tables. Thus, they must withdraw 5.2% ($\frac{1}{19.2}$) of their account in 2001.

Assume the husband dies after taking this distribution. The wife must choose how to treat the inherited IRA. She can take it as a beneficiary and continue to receive payments based upon her single life expectancy. By taking the IRA as her own and naming her grandchild as her beneficiary, she can greatly lengthen the payout schedule.

The grandchild, now age 10, and the grandmother, age 75, have a true combined life expectancy of 71.7 years. But for purposes of computing required IRA withdrawals, a nonspouse beneficiary is treated as being no more than 10 years younger than the IRA owner while the owner lives.

Thus, under IRS tables, the combined life expectancy in 2002 of the now 75-year-old grandmother and the grandchild is considered to be 21.8. The required annual withdrawal the grandmother must make is reduced to 4.6% ($\frac{1}{21.8}$). This smaller withdrawal leaves more money in the account earning tax-deferred income. During the next two years under the special rule, IRS tables give a combined life expectancy for grandmother and grandchild of 20.9 and 20.1 years, requiring annual distributions of 4.8% and 5%.

Assume the grandmother dies in 2004. If she had taken the IRA as a beneficiary, the money remaining in it would be distributed to her estate during the calendar year after her death —and that would have been the end of the IRA.

But because she took the account as her own, the IRA passes to the now 12-year-old grandchild—who can base his/her required withdrawals starting in 2005, at age 13, on the grandchild's life expectancy period, which is 68.8 years. The grandchild need withdraw only 1.5% ($\frac{1}{68.8}$) of the account for the year as his required minimum distribution. Each year thereafter, reduce the divisor by one year. For example, the following year the divisor is 67.8 (68/8 – 1). This withdrawal is so small that the account can be expected to start growing again as a result of investment earnings, and the grandchild can expect to reap tax-deferred earnings in it for the next 68 years!

Bottom line: A person who inherits an IRA from a spouse may elect to treat it as his/her own and may select a beneficiary in order to take advantage of the extended payout rules. The IRS gives an example in which the surviving spouse claims the IRA as her own in the year that the IRA owner dies. In that case, the surviving spouse must select a beneficiary and commence payments by no later than December 31 of the following year. The surviving spouse must create a brand-new IRA and not consolidate it with an old IRA.

Note: The election cannot be made by an executor on behalf of a person who dies before making the election.

Consult with an adviser who is an expert in IRA tax planning for details.

Source: Seymour Goldberg, professor of law and taxation at Long Island University and senior partner in the law firm of Goldberg & Goldberg, PC, 666 Old Country Rd., Garden City, NY 11530. Mr. Goldberg is the author of *A Professional's Guide to the IRA Distribution Rules.* Field Services, New York State Society of Certified Public Accountants.

Build Retirement Wealth In 10 Years with a Defined Benefit Self-Employed Plan

Anyone with self-employment income from personal services, including sideline business income, consultant's fees, freelance income and director's fees, can have a self-employed retirement plan.

They're approved by the IRS, and their tax benefits weren't cut back by tax reform. *Main benefits...*

• Contributions to the plan are tax-deductible.

• Earnings on contributions are not taxed while in the plan.

• Taxes are deferred until retirement, when you are likely to be in a lower tax bracket than you are now.

Problem: Defined contribution self-employed retirement plans—the most common kind of self-employed retirement—won't work for someone who is 50-plus because the most you can put away each year is 13.04% of self-employment income, up to $35,000 in 2001. This is enough for people who have many years to save before retiring, but not for people who are closer to retirement.

Solution: A self-employed defined benefit plan. With defined benefit plans you can put away a much bigger percentage of your income. That's because you are funding an account that is designed to pay you a fixed monthly amount when you retire. So the older you are, the more you can contribute to the plan each year.

They're perfect for someone who has 10 to 15 years to go before retirement.

Opportunity: Because contributions are deducted on your tax return each year, you can shelter large amounts of income during your peak earning years. Money in the account builds up tax-free until withdrawals begin.

How defined benefit plans work: The size of your annual retirement payment is based on a percentage of your salary and the number of years that you have remaining to work before retirement. Next, actuarial tables are used to calculate how much money must be contributed to the defined benefit plan every year.

In 2001 you can set aside enough money in a defined benefit plan to pay you as much as $140,000 a year when you retire. The limit is indexed annually for inflation.

Example: A self-employed 55-year-old sets up a defined benefit plan to provide annual payments of $140,000, the legal maximum, starting at age 65.

Caution: The $140,000 annual limit is reduced if you retire before the Social Security retirement age, from 65 years old to 67 years old depending on the year you were born. Also, the benefit cannot exceed 100% of your average compensation for your highest three consecutive years' earnings.

Drawback: Tax rules are much stricter for defined benefit plans than for defined contribution plans. You must make minimum contributions every year or face a 10% underfunding penalty.

Cost: The defined benefit plan must be custom-made for you by a pension specialist. Expect to pay between $1,000 and $2,000 a year to administer the plan.

Source: Richard A. Imperato, principal, KPMG, LLP, 345 Park Ave., New York 10154.

The Biggest Traps in Retirement Planning

To make the most of your retirement years, start planning now. The earlier you start, the more you will be able to achieve.

Set Goals

The first mistake of retirement planning is not having goals. When you don't know what you want, you are *un*likely to attain it. *Helpful:* Draw up a "dream list" for your retirement years. *Consider…*

•Where you will want to live.

•Your desired lifestyle.

•The income you will need.

•The specific steps required to turn as much of the list as possible into reality.

Goal-Setting Requires You to…

•Take action. By having a goal of a certain amount of savings by a fixed date, you know how much you must save each year starting now. This also shows you how costly it is to delay saving, giving a greater incentive to start saving right away.

Example: Put away just $50 a month starting at age 25 and, assuming an average 5% after-tax annual return, you'll have $76,619 saved by age 65—at $100 a month, your nest egg will be $153,238. By contrast, put away the same $50 a month starting at age 55, and you'll have just $7,796 by age 65…$100 a month will yield only $15,593.

•Be realistic. Everybody wants many things, but goal-setting makes you decide what's most important. Once you decide this, you can begin to assess how much money you're going to need. But more than finances are involved here. You're more likely to be happy in your retirement years if you've achieved what's important to you than if you've left your dreams too vague to be realized.

•Be consistent. People typically want two things from their retirement investments— safety for their savings and big returns to fund a comfortable retirement lifestyle. But, of course, there's an inherent conflict here.

A sound investment plan designed to meet specific goals will make the most of the trade-off between risk and opportunity and enable you to avoid the costly and common mistakes of investing either too riskily or with too much caution.

Example: You might invest in aggressive growth stocks while retirement is still years away, knowing that if the stock market falls there will be plenty of time for your portfolio to recover. Then, as retirement nears, you can shift money gradually into safer investments. With a specific financial target, you will know how much to shift each year to guarantee security. Excess funds can remain invested aggressively in the hope of hitting a financial "home run." The chance of big gains remains while risk is minimized.

Key: The target retirement date you set will have a big impact on planning strategies and the amount you must save each year.

Pick a date that is sooner rather than later. If you work beyond your planned retirement date, the extra income will simply make you even better off. But if you are forced to retire early, you will be glad to have planned for it. And it will always be pleasant to have the option of retiring early if you want to.

To Avoid Other Common Mistakes

•Understand your company's retirement plan. Most people don't. *Ask:*

•How do benefits differ if you are terminated, take early retirement or leave at the normal retirement age?

•What would happen if you left the company today?

•Is there a vesting schedule that requires you to stay with the company a set number of years in order to receive full benefits?

•Will you receive a fixed pension with a dollar value you can estimate now? Or does the company have a profit-sharing plan under which its contribution to your account varies each year, making your final benefit an uncertain amount?

•Are plan benefits adjusted in line with inflation? If not, you may need extra income.

•How and when will you get paid? Plan payouts may not occur until months after you retire. And if a company has more than one plan, they may make payouts at different times. This can drastically affect personal cash flow, so anticipate a retirement plan's red tape.

Warning: Beware of plan modifications. Many firms are cutting back retirement benefits to save costs. Employees must be notified when their retirement plan is modified, so pay attention and be sure you understand changes that affect you.

•Understand Social Security. Figure your expected benefit in advance. *Helpful:* Contact your local Social Security office and ask them to compute your expected benefit for you.

Big trap: Most people expect that they will receive their pension and Social Security. But many companies have "integrated" plans under which the designated pension amount includes Social Security—the company's contribution toward your pension is reduced by the amount of Social Security you receive. Find out whether your company's plan is integrated or not.

Social Security options: Some firms allow workers to retire early—before they are eligible to receive Social Security. Those companies increase early pension payments by the amount of the monthly Social Security that the retiree will ultimately receive. When Social Security payments start, pension payments are reduced accordingly. The result is an even flow of income to the employee that can facilitate early-retirement planning.

Consider taking Social Security benefits early, at age 62, instead of your normal retirement age. While waiting until your normal retirement age provides a larger monthly benefit, you also miss more than three years of payments in the meantime, and it can take many years of increased monthly payments to make up this difference.

If you retire before age 65 but continue to work, full-time or part-time, consider postponing collecting benefits until age 65. If you're under 65 and earn more than a threshold amount ($10,680 in 2001), you'll lose $1 in benefits for each $2 of earnings over the threshold. But, once you reach 65, you can earn any amount without a loss of benefits.

•Make full use of company life insurance. Some companies have group policies that allow departing employees to convert their term insurance into whole life coverage without going through a physical examination. If your company offers this benefit, don't overlook it. If this benefit isn't offered, be aware that when you are older it may be more difficult to pass a required physical to get insurance. If you will need coverage then, take steps to secure it now.

•Consider health insurance. Figure out in advance what the cost of insurance will be after you retire. Ask if your company provides retirement health benefits, and what the plan limits

are. If you will have to pay for your own coverage, figure it in as a cost of retirement and start saving for it now.

Ask now about nursing-home insurance and Medigap insurance for expenses not covered by Medicare, so that if the day comes in retirement that you need to obtain such coverage you will be familiar with it. Don't make the mistake of thinking, "It won't happen to me."

•Protect yourself as a spouse. *Ask:* What are your rights under your spouse's retirement program? Has your spouse selected a survivorship option, so benefits will continue to be paid to you should he/she die first? Do you know where all necessary documents are located in the event your spouse dies or becomes incapacitated? What will happen to benefits in the event of divorce?

Note: Alimony is considered compensation and can be used to make IRA contributions.

Important: The worst time to make serious financial decisions is while experiencing the trauma of the loss of a spouse. Do financial planning beforehand so you will know what to do if or when the day comes.

•Diversify wealth. It's dangerous to keep all your wealth in one investment as retirement nears. Yet many people do so, especially sole proprietors and executives who keep their money in their own businesses.

Better: As retirement draws near, spread funds among several investments so that your retirement position won't be endangered by a loss suffered in any one area.

•Consider a lump-sum distribution. When you retire, it may be advantageous to take your benefit in the form of a lump-sum payment, rather than through annual pension or annuity payments. This gives you investment control over your money. A lump-sum distribution may be rolled over into an IRA tax-free if deposited within 60 days of receipt. The money must be transferred directly from the company plan to the IRA to avoid a 20% withholding tax on the payout.

There's a tax break for a lump-sum distribution in the form of income averaging—treating it as if it were received over a period of 10 years if you were born before 1936. The result is that much of the distribution avoids being taxed at top-bracket rates. Technical rules apply, so consult with your tax adviser about making the right choices.

•Consider taking money out of an IRA before age 59½ without paying an early withdrawal penalty. This is possible if payouts are taken in the form of an annuity—that is, in even payments over your life expectancy—or to pay medical expenses that exceed 7.5% of your Adjusted Gross Income, health insurance if you're unemployed, first-time home-buying expenses or higher education costs.

•Do the paperwork. Make sure, for example, that all beneficiaries are properly designated or survivor benefits may not be paid out according to your wishes.

•Get qualified advice. Both investment advice and tax advice are absolute musts. Remember, you're planning your future and managing your life savings, so seek out the most qualified experts that you can find.

Source: Anna Polizzi-Keller, tax partner in the financial counseling and expatriate (citizens based outside the country of their citizenship) areas, Ernst & Young, 701 Market St., St. Louis 63101.

Run Personal Finances Like a Business

Most executives neglect their personal finances because they are too busy with their jobs or businesses. That's a serious mistake. *Stay alert for opportunities to save and profit:*

•Pension plans. Business owners and the self-employed can take advantage of special pension options open to them. If you are making $100,000 a year, you could easily put away $30,000 pre-tax into a defined benefit pension plan. Greater earnings may justify even larger contributions. Compounding tax-free dollars gives an enormous investment edge.

•A favorite tax-planning tactic is to have a minor child work for the family-owned business. The first $4,550 earned by the child in 2001 is tax-free, and further income is taxed at low rates. In addition, the company gets a deduction for the child's salary. A dramatic taxpayer victory shows just how effective this tactic can be:

The taxpayers owned a mobile-home park and hired their three children, ages 7, 11 and 12, to work there. The children cleaned the grounds, did landscaping work, maintained the swimming pool, answered phones and did minor repair work. The taxpayers deducted over $17,000 that they paid to the children during a three-year period. But the IRS objected, and the case went to trial. *Court's decision:* Over $15,000 of deductions were approved. Most of the deductions that were disallowed were attributable to the 7-year-old. But even $1,200 of his earnings were approved by the court.

Key: The children actually performed the work for which they were paid. And the work was necessary for the business. The taxpayers demonstrated that if their children had not done the work, they would have had to hire someone else to do it.

Types of jobs children could do: Write checks or send out bills for your business, do simple maintenance and painting for investment real estate you own, etc.

•Set a spouse up in business. Most executives don't realize the tax benefits they could get from encouraging their spouses to start a business. *Some of the benefits:*

•As long as the business shows a profit for three of the first five years, the IRS generally won't challenge the right to deduct losses in the other two years. These losses can be offset directly against the high-earner's high-tax-bracket income.

•If the spouse's business travel plans coincide with those of the executive, travel costs are mostly deductible. (Of course, a business trip can also coincide with vacation travel. But be sure it's predominantly business travel.)

•The spouse can be covered by the business's retirement plan. Also the spouse can invest up to $2,000 of earned income in an IRA. Whether to claim a deduction or use the Roth IRA depends on the couple's income and other factors.

•Three-generation financial planning. Consider asking your parents to transfer some of their wealth directly to your children. (*Easiest way to skip a generation:* Each grandparent gives each grandchild $10,000 a year in tax-free gifts.)

•Supporting elderly parents. If you are self-employed, consider employing your parent in the business. *Opportunities:* Write the monthly checks. Manage a piece of real estate. Investigate any investment you are considering.

Special concern: If your parent is under 65 and receives Social Security benefits, he or she will lose $1 of Social Security for every $2 earned over a certain amount. *One way around this:* Set up an S corporation with the parent as stockholder. The dividends paid out of the S corporation do not diminish Social Security payments. Of course, once the parent reaches 65, no earnings affect Social Security payments.

Caution: The Social Security Administration has authority under the law to look beyond the facade of a business enterprise and determine the true situation. It is possible that if it finds the corporation was established solely to avoid deduction of Social Security benefits, it can impose deductions against benefits.

Pension Benefits

The bottom line in retirement planning today: Don't count benefits that you've been counting on. With general restructuring and cost-cutting efforts, many companies have been finding ways to terminate or reduce their pension obligations. *Changes to watch out for:* Companies often take workers' Social Security payments into account when figuring pension benefits. They reason that since they paid half of those premiums, they're entitled to reduce their share of your defined benefits by half of whatever you'll be receiving from Social Security.

Problem: Most employees think of their pension benefits as separate from Social Security. *Somewhat helpful:* The Tax Act of 1986 specified that in most cases employers can't subtract more than 50% of your pension benefits, regardless of how much you receive from Social Security.

Protection: Ask your employer annually for a benefits statement showing how much you would receive at retirement if you left the company now or at various points in the future. You'll find, for example, that if you were to retire at 55 instead of at 65, most companies would cut your pension benefits in half. Be sure to ask for the figures with and without salary increases, since those are, of course, not guaranteed.

Never assume that pension benefit projections will hold up 100%. Often they turn out to have been too optimistic. *Goal:* To replace at least 50%–70% of your final salary. That's considered a minimum for living in relative comfort during retirement.

Source: Kenneth P. Shapiro, president, Hay/Huggins Co., Inc., the benefits and actuarial consulting subsidiary of Hay Group, 229 S. 18 St., Philadelphia 19103.

How Safe Is Your Pension?

More and more people are discovering—to their horror—that they can't rely solely on their company defined benefit pension plan for retirement security. Some companies have even terminated plans or changed to cash balance defined benefit plans that provide smaller benefits to older, long-term workers. And sometimes plans fail because of a company's financial problems or problems with an insurance company that provided a guaranteed income contract.

What can you do? Not much, if a pension-plan failure catches you unprepared. You could write to the US Department of Labor, but in practice it can't be counted on to do much unless you're with a large company. Nor is the IRS likely to provide much help. The Pension Benefits Guaranty Corporation is supposed to pay when defined benefit plans fail, but it has payout caps that could be much less than what you were counting on, and some observers claim the organization is overextended. Nearly all lawyers with pension-plan expertise work for plan sponsors, not individual participants.

Avoid Bad Surprises

Keep yourself informed about your company's pension plan. Ask yourself fundamental questions…

• What's the pension plan invested in?

• Is the pension portfolio heavily loaded with your company's stocks?

• Is the pension plan in sound condition?

• If your company offers a guaranteed income contract portfolio, is it provided by a single insurer? If just one, how solid is it?

• How sound is your company? Monitor annual reports, quarterly reports and business news affecting your company.

• What are the ratings of insurance companies involved with your guaranteed income contract portfolio? Consider a B- (or lower) rating from A.M. Best, Moody's or Standard & Poor's as a warning flag.

Self-Defense

• Consider a pension plan as one part of an overall portfolio. Don't rely on a company pension plan to provide the bulk of your retirement assets. Put eligible funds into an IRA. Build your own portfolio of savings and investments.

Your portfolio should be properly diversified, enabling you to survive in the event that something goes awry. Diversification is especially important for the millions of people who acquired large chunks of their company's stock through employee stock-ownership plans. If you have more than 5% to 10% of your assets in a single stock, look to diversify your portfolio.

• Think ahead about healthcare. Because costs are escalating dramatically, more and more companies are curtailing dollar payouts in many ways. You might not be able to use the doctor or hospital of your choice unless you pay out-of-pocket. Set aside additional savings for adequate healthcare protection or consider other forms of health insurance appropriate for your circumstances.

Source: George E.L. Barbee, executive director, client services, Price Waterhouse, 1251 Avenue of the Americas, New York 10020. He is a contributor to the *Price Waterhouse Retirement Adviser.* Pocket Books.

Pension Traps—Annuity Opportunities

Before collecting checks from your company pension plan or a single-premium deferred annuity, it pays to investigate your options.

By choosing an immediate annuity, you may wind up with hundreds of dollars more per month in your pocket—at no additional risk.

An immediate annuity is an insurance contract that, in return for a one-time payment, starts paying a fixed sum for your lifetime or for some other period right away.

A single-life annuity, for example, pays the agreed-upon sum every month until the purchaser dies. The payment doesn't have to stop at the first death. It depends on the option you select: Joint and two-thirds survivor, joint and 50% survivor, and joint and 100% survivor. A joint-and-survivor annuity for a married couple, by contrast, pays one larger sum while both spouses are alive and a lesser amount after the first spouse dies. Payments continue at the lower level during the lifetime of the surviving spouse and end only when that person dies.

It Pays to Shop

Comparison shopping in the immediate annuity market can pay off quite nicely.

Example: Recently, I checked out rates—which are expressed as monthly income per $10,000 of premium—for a 65-year-old woman. For a $100,000 investment, the monthly income ranged from a high of $915 to a low of $716—a difference of almost $200, or about 28%.

Trap: Don't automatically go for the highest monthly income figure. Given all the turmoil in the insurance industry these days, and the failure of Executive Life, in the example above I decided not even to consider the seven companies paying the top rates because I had reservations about their soundness. Bear in mind that you are purchasing something that you intend to last for the rest of your life.

I wound up recommending my client purchase an annuity that ranked 20th out of 100. It was offered by Northwestern Mutual, the solid, conservative and well-run Minnesota company. The annuity provided monthly income of $839. The median income figure was $809 a month.

Compare Carefully

Two common situations in which investigating what you'd receive with an immediate annuity makes sense...

•When you're retiring from your company. Before you automatically accept the monthly pension check your company plan offers, ask if the plan permits a lump-sum distribution instead. Many, but not all, plans do.

See what you can get in monthly income by purchasing an immediate annuity with some of that money. You may be surprised to discover that you'll get a much larger payment with the annuity than with your company pension.

•When you're ready to start annuitizing, or receiving distributions, from a single-premium deferred annuity that you purchased years ago. Just because you purchased the annuity from Company A, don't assume that it now offers the best deal in terms of monthly income. You may do better by switching to Company B or C.

Caution: In either case, don't sink all your money into an immediate annuity all at once. You may be purchasing at a trough, and annuity rates may subsequently shoot up. I recommend that people purchase several contracts over time and that they not annuitize more than 50% of their total investable assets.

It's vital that you do your comparative shopping right at the point when you are ready to make your purchase.

Reason: The immediate annuity market is a very fluid one, and rates can fluctuate widely, even within a given company, depending upon the details of your individual situation.

Example: A particular company may post attractive payouts one month, but not the next. Or, it may be competitive at some ages but unattractive at others.

To check on the different rates offered by different companies, consult *Best's Retirement Income Guide.* It's published twice a year and is available in many public libraries. The guide contains comparative information on many different types of annuities, both fixed and variable, offered by hundreds of different companies.

To find out the annuity rate for an immediate annuity, you must consult the tables in the back, which give the monthly income you would receive if you pay a set sum to different insurance companies queried.

It's also possible to deal with a reputable broker who maintains a broad database of annuity rates paid by different companies. *Sources:*

•The Annuity Network, a subsidiary of the Laughlin Group in Beaverton, Oregon. The parent company evaluates the safety and stability of insurance companies. The Annuity Network works with about 300 insurance companies. The network is compensated on a commission basis from companies whose policies it sells.

•United States Annuities, Monroe Township, New Jersey. An insurance-brokerage and research firm that specializes in immediate annuities. It also works on a commission basis. The firm publishes the *Annuity Shopper*, a bimonthly newsletter that compares different insurers' ratings, rates and charges.

Of course, there are some drawbacks to opting for an immediate annuity rather than for your company pension. Rejecting your pension might be unwise, for example, if your company has a history of increasing its pension payouts from time to time in order to offset inflation. The annuity check you get the first month is the same amount you'll receive 20 years from now —assuming you're still alive to collect.

And—pensions are insured by the Pension Board Guaranty Corporation, while immediate annuities are only as good as the company that issues them.

Before you jump at the highest available rate, you should always very carefully investigate the issuing company's financial health.

Aim: To be reasonably sure it will be able to make those payouts as long as you live.

Caution: Some, but not all, insurers require annuity buyers to pay upfront policy fees or other charges, which can range from $150 to $500. And about 10 states impose premium taxes that amount to 1% to 3% of the amount invested.

Source: Glenn Daily, a fee-only insurance consultant and author of *The Individual Investor's Guide to Low-Load Insurance Products.* International Publishing Corp.

Borrow from Your Pension Plan

Did you know that you can usually borrow from your pension plan? You must repay the loan in level payments over no more than five years (longer if you borrow to buy a home). Also, you must pay interest on the loan at the going rate. There are limitations on the maximum amounts that can be borrowed as follows:

Vested Portion in Pension Plan	Maximum Amount of Borrowing
Up to $20,000	50% of amount of plan
Over $20,000	50% up to $50,000 maximum amount

Source: *New Tax Traps/New Opportunities* by Edward Mendlowitz, CPA. Boardroom Special Reports.

Benefits of Early Retirement

Collecting Social Security early can pay off. Even though benefits are reduced, they'll usually add up to more in the long run.

Example: If full benefits are $750 per month for retiring at age 65, you can get reduced benefits of $600 a month by retiring at age 62. You'd have to collect full benefits for 12 years to make up the $21,600 you'd receive during the three years of early payments.

Caution: As the normal retirement age increases over 65, the reduction in benefits for retiring at age 62 also increases.

Source: *Changing Times*, Washington, DC.

IRAs...to Consolidate... Or Not Consolidate?

Taxpayers who have set up a number of IRAs over the years may be tempted to gather them together into one big IRA. There are definite advantages to consolidating accounts:

•Save on trustees' fees. Instead of paying separate administration fees for each account, you'll be paying only one.

•Simplify paperwork.

•Accumulate larger balances for investment. You get a greater rate of return on a $10,000 Certificate of Deposit (CD) than on a $1,000 CD.

Main disadvantage in consolidating IRA accounts: Problems with early withdrawals. When you consolidate accounts, you lose flexibility in making penalty-free early withdrawals.

Source: Deborah Walker, partner, KPMG, LLP, 2001 M St. NW, Washington, DC 20036.

CHAPTER TWO

Investment Opportunities

Avoiding the Biggest Mistakes Investors Make

Basic Mistakes

•*Mistake:* Not considering taxes until you begin preparing tax returns. By then it's often too late to adopt strategies that could have cut the tax bill. Monitor the tax implications of your investments throughout the year and periodically consult with your accountant.

•*Mistake:* Failing to take responsibility for tax and investment strategies. Some investors rely completely on accountants, brokers, lawyers or other advisers. Of course, you should seek advice from tax and investment professionals and use their expertise when implementing the strategies you decide upon. But it's important to remember that you are the person who will have to live with the results, so take responsibility and begin planning ahead now to make the most of your investments.

•*Mistake:* Not quantifying tax consequences when comparing investment options. This means looking at the dollar numbers earned after taxes from investments that receive different tax treatment.

This example is simpler than most real cases. Some investments are partially taxable—for example, US Treasury issues are exempt from state tax but not from federal tax. Also, your own tax bracket will vary according to local law, income level and the deductions and credits available to you.

In some cases, it may pay to increase tax exposure.

Example: If you live in a low- or no-tax state, it may pay to move funds from Treasury bonds to a portfolio of AAA-grade corporate bonds, to receive more income after taxes with almost the same safety, even though more total tax will be due.

The way to know which investment plan is best for you is to work through the numbers illustrating different options.

•*Mistake:* Not making full use of retirement plans. Tax-favored retirement programs let you obtain the higher returns offered by taxable investments in a tax-deferred environment. Today, personal retirement accounts such as IRAs, SEPs, SIMPLEs and self-employed retire-ment plans can invest in almost anything except collectibles, mortgaged rental properties or a business in which you own an interest of 5% or more. Employer-provided 401(k) savings plans also offer self-directed investment options.

Common mistake: Thinking the main tax benefit from a retirement-plan contribution is the deduction for it and making contributions at the last minute each year. In fact, over the long run, the tax-deferral obtained for compound retirement-plan earnings can be more valuable than the contribution deduction.

Example: A $2,000 traditional IRA contribution saves $800 for a person in a 40% combined federal and state tax bracket. But a contribution made early in the year will also earn tax-deferred income within the account during the year. If the IRA earns 10%, $2,000 contributed a year before the deadline for just one year will earn $200, and over 30 years this $200 will compound to $3,490—all of which is forfeited if you make your contribution at the last minute instead. If this contribution is made early each year, the increase in total retirement funds available is significant.

Make plan contributions as early in the year as possible.

Alternatively, consider making nondeductible Roth IRA contributions if eligible to do so. While there's no current tax deduction, earnings will be tax-free if certain conditions are met.

Estate-Planning Mistake

Not averting estate taxes is a big mistake. Many people put off estate planning simply because thinking about death is not pleasant. Others underestimate the cost of estate taxes because they believe the $675,000 applicable exclusion amount for 2001 will protect them, or because they know they can pass assets tax-free to a spouse. *Alert:* The applicable exclusion amount will increase in stages to $1 million by 2006. *Traps:*

•Your estate may be pushed far over the $675,000 amount by assets that you don't think of—such as life-insurance proceeds, the value of retirement accounts or appreciation in the value of your home.

•Passing all your assets to your spouse can be a costly mistake, because he/she will be able to pass no more than $675,000 in 2001 to the next generation tax-free—while the two of you could plan together to pass a combined $1.35 million.

•*Self-defense:* Have the insurance on your life owned by your spouse, a child or a trust benefiting family members. You can provide the money needed to pay the premiums through annual tax-free gifts. When you die, the insurance proceeds will not be part of your taxable estate.

•*Self-defense:* If your assets exceed $675,000 in 2001, make double use of the $650,000 unified estate-and-gift-tax applicable exclusion amount by passing up to $675,000 of your assets to children directly. *Alternative:* Use a trust that pays income to your spouse for life and then distributes its assets to your children, while leaving the remainder of your assets to your spouse. The $675,000 exclusion amount will be available both for your disposition of property and for your spouse's disposition of property inherited from you.

•*Self-defense:* Use gifts to cut your estate. You can make gifts of up to $10,000 each to as many separate recipients as you wish annually, free of gift tax. The limit is $20,000 if the gift is made jointly with your spouse. You can also make larger tax-free gifts by using part of your unified credit. Although this will reduce the amount of the credit that will be available to your estate, it can pay off if you expect the gift assets to appreciate in value before you die.

Gifts of income-producing assets to family members in lower income-tax brackets, such as children over age 14, can cut family income taxes as well. And gifts of appreciated assets to low-bracket family members can be cashed in by these family members with less gains tax resulting.

Strategy: When older family members have less than $675,000 in assets, a reverse gift can save big taxes. You can make gifts to them of assets that have appreciated in value. When they die, the assets will pass back to you or to other family members with stepped-up basis —revalued for tax purposes at market value— so potential gains tax on their appreciation is eliminated.

More Tax-Cutting Ideas

•Earmark stock and mutual-fund shares to maximize the tax advantage when shares are sold.

Example: Say you bought shares in a stock or mutual fund at different times at different prices and now wish to sell some. If you have price records for specific shares, you can sell the particular shares that produce the optimal gain or loss—perhaps to minimize taxable gain or to maximize a capital loss that will protect other gains from tax. If you do not have price records, the IRS will treat the first shares bought as the first sold.

•Get the IRS to absorb part of the sales load on a mutual fund. Do this by buying shares in a money fund offered by a family of funds. After three months or more, transfer out of the money fund and into one of the other fund options (stocks, bonds, etc.). The sales load will produce a loss on the sale of the money-fund shares, which you can deduct or use to shelter other gains from tax.

•Look for losses in your portfolio that can be used to offset gains or generate deductions.

Tactic: Use tax swaps to produce paper losses that can shelter gains from tax. *How:* Sell a security to produce a loss, then immediately buy back a similar (but not identical) security.

Example: You can sell a bond and then buy back a bond from a different issuer that pays the same interest and has the same maturity date and credit rating. You get a loss deduction while maintaining your investment position. You cannot buy back the same security within 30 days to produce a tax loss.

The 30-day time limit does not apply if you sell a security to produce a gain. So if you already have a loss, you can sell a security at a gain, shelter the gain with the loss, then immediately buy back the same security, avoiding future tax that would otherwise have been due on its appreciation.

•Consider "trader" status. If you actively manage your portfolio to profit from market swings—instead of profiting from appreciation, and dividend and interest payments—you may qualify as a professional stock trader and become eligible to deduct investment costs on Schedule C as business expenses. This enables you to fully deduct items which provide only limited deductions to investors, such as interest and investment expenses.

Although you cannot make deductible contributions to SEP, SIMPLE or other self-employed retirement plans from trading gains, trading gains are not subject to self-employment taxes either. Consult your tax adviser about how the rules may apply to your situation.

Source: Ted Tesser, CPA, 30 Waterside Plaza #9G, New York 10010. His firm, Waterside Financial Services, assists clients with tax, investment and retirement-plan strategies. He is author of *The Serious Investor's Tax Survival Guide*, which includes a free tax update, *Maximizing Profit Under the Clinton Administration*. Traders' Library.

When to Get Out of A Mutual Fund

To check your fund holdings for "lemons," look at the quarterly Lipper Analytical Services mutual fund data. These are reported in many newspapers and financial publications. Guidelines to use...

•Make proper comparisons. Measure your fund's performance against funds with a similar investment objective.

Example: Don't compare against the Standard & Poor's 500 Index unless yours is an index fund with the same objective.

•Use meaningful time periods. Check your fund's relative performance against its peer average for one year, three years and five years.

Reason: Any fund manager can have a bad quarter, and that's not necessarily a reason to dump the fund.

First cut: Funds that have been underperforming for all three periods.

Second cut: Funds that are marginal performers—or worse—and charge more in annual fees than the average in their peer group. *Benchmark:* The average fee for a domestic stock fund is 80 basis points (0.80%).

Third cut: If you are fairly heavily invested in growth, capital appreciation or index funds where you have substantial profits but are concerned about a market correction, lower your risk by moving some of those assets into balanced funds and/or growth-and-income funds.

Caution: Consider the tax consequences of any sale carefully.

Source: Doug Fabian, president, Fabian Investment Resources, a mutual-fund advisory service in Huntington Beach, California. *Fabian's Lemon List* of expensive, underperforming mutual funds is available free on-line at www.fabian.com.

How to Get Out of a Guaranteed Investment Contract Trap

The troubled condition of several large insurance companies raises concern among many conservative, long-term investors in annuities and guaranteed investment contracts (GICs) about the safety of those holdings.

GICs and annuities written by insurance companies have been heavily used to fund retirement accounts.

•GICs. These contracts between an employer and an insurance company to pay a fixed rate of return for a set number of years have attracted more than two thirds of the estimated $125 billion in company 401(k) savings plans.

•Deferred annuities. Deferred annuities have been aggressively marketed by insurance companies to individuals in recent years as tax-deferred retirement investment accounts.

Takeover trap: Thousands of employees found their long-standing company pensions converted into annuities when their companies were taken over. New, financially slick managements identified hidden assets in "overfunded" pension accounts, took out the surplus, terminated conventional pension plans and bought annuities to cover remaining pension liabilities.

The problems of GIC and annuity investors suddenly became apparent...

•GICs are not very guaranteed. The "guarantee" by the insurance company applies to the rate of interest—not the investment itself. Protection of principal is dependent on the financial condition of the insurance company. Executive Life Insurance Co., seized by California insurance regulators in April 1991, had sold about $3 billion in GICs. Thus far the company's conservators have not paid anything on these contracts—though they are fully paying out death benefits on Executive Life's life insurance policies.

•Annuity trap. The Pension Guaranty Corporation, created under the Employee Retirement Income Security Act (ERISA) to insure pension plans, does not guarantee the annuities employees may be left with once a company terminates the pension plan.

•No GIC defender. The life insurance industry's guarantee programs, organized on a state-by-state basis to protect policy holders when an insurance company gets into financial trouble, show little eagerness to cover GICs.

•Annuity defense. Many—but not all—insurance industry guarantee programs cover annuities. So far, the California State Insurance Department is paying only 70 cents on the $1 to Executive Life annuity holders.

GIC Options

What individuals who have substantial savings in GICs can do:

•Immediately ask the company benefit manager which insurance companies are behind the GICs in your company's 401(k) plan. (Except for the very smallest plans, most companies negotiated contracts with more than one insurance company to diversify risk.)

•Ask the company benefit manager for the most current rating of those insurance companies. *Least risk for you:* The companies that are top rated—A+ for the A.M. Best rating service and A+ for Weiss Research…AAA for Standard & Poor's and Duff & Phelps…Aaa for Moody's.

•If the insurers are not top-rated by at least two—preferably three—of these rating agencies, express your concern and ask what the company is doing to move to a less risky carrier.

Ask specifically: Does the GIC contract have a liquidity feature?

This would enable the company to get out of the contract—usually at a penalty. That would reduce the value of the invested funds—a loss for the employees invested in the GIC. And a new GIC contract would probably pay a lower rate of interest.

•If you have a substantial sum invested in the GIC option of your company savings plan and find it is "guaranteed" by an insurance company that is not top-rated, seriously consider diversifying your investment into other plan options. *Likely limitation:* Many company savings plans that offer a GIC option do not have another fixed-income option, such as a money-market fund or a bond fund. Your only other option may be a stock fund or company stock. You will have to assess whether a move to equities opens the door to more risk than you potentially face in the GIC.

Annuity Options

Individuals who have purchased annuities should also ask their brokers to provide specific ratings information on the insurance company behind the annuity.

Anthony Amodeo, vice president of Metropolitan Life, a top-rated insurance company, explains what options individuals with substantial investments in annuities backed by low-rated insurers have. If you are one of those whose company pension has been transferred to an annuity, there's nothing that you can do to move to another company.

And your options are nil, too, if you made a major lump-sum investment in an immediate annuity—one that pays you a set amount until death.

But you probably don't have to lose too much sleep over these accounts.

State insurance guarantee associations either cover annuities of failed insurance companies or are showing a disposition to cover them when a problem surfaces, even if their regulations don't yet require it.

Deferred annuities: You do have options with deferred annuities. Look at the plan's surrender charges. Typically, such plans have a maximum surrender charge—say about 7% of the total value of the annuity—if you cancel the annuity in the first, second or third years. After that the surrender charge diminishes, eventually to zero for most. *Factors you must balance in deciding whether or not to withdraw from such an annuity:*

•Surrender penalty, if any.

•Income-tax liability, if any, on the withdrawn funds.

It might be possible to defer taxes by transferring to another annuity.

But IRS rules on annuity withdrawals are tricky. Make sure you get professional tax advice.

•The possible loss of a tax-deferred investment.

•Opportunities that you perceive in putting your money into an alternative investment.

Source: Several insurance industry insiders.

Investment Lessons

There's no shortage of financial advice on Wall Street. The problem is that much of this financial advice is conflicting and leaves individuals confused or stuck in bad investments. So what's an investor to do?

Decisions/Decisions

•"Buy low and sell high" is sound financial advice—but there are actually four decisions to make. Stock-market experts like to say that timing is everything, and most investors strive to sell at the top of a market and buy at the bottom.

This strategy is also known as the "contrary opinion"—doing the opposite of what most other investors are doing at a given time.

But moving successfully against the crowd is very difficult.

Trap: Market cycles contain many small, deceptive movements—so the buy-sell phases aren't always clear. *Here are five decisions a contrarian investor must make…*

•When the market is approaching the bottom of a cycle, sellers no longer have the stomach to buy. This creates an opportunity for bargain hunters. To determine when the market has reached this point, you can evaluate stocks using historically low valuations of revenues, earnings and dividends. Or you can wait for an uptrend before buying.

•After you buy, don't sell immediately after the bull trend becomes obvious to everyone. Let the crowd join you as the movement upward progresses.

•When serious overvaluation is reached, go against the majority and sell. Determine this moment by setting a price objective beforehand. Or base your timing on the heat of the market. Wait for the first sign of market weakness.

•As the downward cycle advances, resist the temptation to buy back your stock at a lower price. Wait until the market approaches the bottom again before buying.

•Don't confuse portfolio activity with progress toward investment goals. A common mistake made by many investors is rapid portfolio activity. They regard time as the enemy and believe that if they wait too long, that is an invitation for something to go wrong.

It's unrealistic, however, to expect that instant profits are easy to grab. When too much attention is focused on achieving short-term goals, the real opportunity—which is long-term—is forgotten. Think of time as an ally, not as an enemy.

•Beware of the company that offers creative excuses for underachievement. Some companies have a talent for making excuses for problems. Be especially wary of companies that wrap bad news in good news. *Danger signs:*

•When shortfalls and disappointments come with good-news announcements, such as the introduction of a new product or overhead-reduction programs.

•When you find your mailbox jammed with "We love you, shareholder" letters from the company.

•When bad news is accompanied by an announcement of a management shake-up. Did the company also say what took so long for them to clean up the problem? If not, incompetents may still be in charge.

Once credibility has been destroyed, it takes a long time for a company to win it back. When management repeatedly says, "Things will be better next year," it's time to sell.

•Focus on essentials…skip the merely interesting. Experienced investors are humble. They've learned that they can't possibly know everything. Less seasoned investors, on the other hand, may feel that if they had only a few more hours to do research, their investment returns would be considerably better. Usually this is hogwash.

Save time by not seeking out the opinions of yet another expert. Formulating intelligent questions that you then go out and seek answers to is much more valuable than collecting opinions.

Focus on an industry's prospects, the strength and track record of a company and the long-term implications of a new development.

•Good corporate news can lead to a dangerous sense of euphoria. When there's good news, companies can't wait to circulate it. Many ladle it out in advance, tipping off key stock-market analysts. The result is that these stocks often rise before the news hits the media and afterward rise only slightly—or even fall.

Reasons: Many pros "sell on the news"—or take profits as the news becomes widely known and the price rises—and companies often use good news as an opportunity to seek more equity financing.

Similarly, beware of remarkably upbeat presentations at investment conferences. Instead, wait a few weeks or a month, and you'll almost always be able to buy the stock cheaper.

Opportunity: Look at the volume in the weeks before an "announcement." If it's high, this tells you that you may be late in getting the word.

•Study the composition of a company's board of directors. The role of a company's board of directors is to represent the interests of all stockholders. One way to determine whether the directors are representing your interests is to look at the people who make up the board. *How to tell a good board from a bad one…*

•Determine how many directors come from the company and how many are from the outside. If most are from the inside, the board may not be independent enough to resist undue pressure from top management.

•Examine the credentials of the outsiders. If they are not particularly distinguished, they may have been chosen as "good buddies."

•If the board is small—fewer than five members—it's likely that outside directors were chosen for their cooperative attitude toward management preferences. On the other hand, a large board—more than 10—is probably too unwieldy to support much independence on the part of outside directors.

•The company's proxy statement will reveal the extent of each director's stock ownership and options and interest in the future of the company. Token holdings are danger signs.

•Learn to distinguish the truly underappreciated stock from the real losers. *Key question:* Is the stock misunderstood by Wall Street or is it more likely that management misunderstands what's happened to its market?

Don't be fooled by a company's aura or unduly impressed by its past glories. "What have you done for me lately?" is a legitimate question to ask. "What do you plan to do tomorrow?" is an even better one.

Don't jettison a stock simply because it's the biggest loser in your portfolio. That's a short-term balm that usually turns into a long-term mistake.

Source: George Stasen, a venture-capital expert and chief operating officer of Supra Medical Corp., and Robert Metz, a financial journalist. They are coauthors of *It's a Sure Thing: A Wry Look at Investing, Investors and the World of Wall Street.* McGraw-Hill.

Loopholes for Investors

One type of income that is taxed at beneficial rates is long-term capital-gain income. This income generally is taxed at a top rate of 20% today (10% for those in the 15% tax bracket)—nearly half the top rate on other income.

•*Loophole:* Make full use of capital losses. Losses on the sale of securities are fully deductible against gains. If your losses exceed your gains, up to $3,000 of those excess losses are deductible each year against your salary and other income. Unused losses that you can't deduct because of the $3,000 limit can be carried forward to future tax years until they are used up.

•*Loophole:* Buy stock in a mutual fund before it makes a capital-gain distribution. This is a way of "creating" capital gains. The distribution to you is capital-gain income. You can offset that income with losses you've accumulated from other sales. That way you won't pay tax on the distribution.

•*Loophole:* Give appreciated securities to your children instead of selling the securities and giving the children cash. This is a tax-smart way to come up with money for education expenses for a child who is older than 13. If you sell the securities yourself, you'll pay tax on any long-term gains. But if you give the securities to the child and let him/her sell them, the gain could be taxed at the child's lower rate, which could be 10% or zero.

•*Loophole:* Give appreciated securities to charity. When you do this, you get an income-tax deduction for the full fair market value of the securities at the time of the gift, and you don't pay tax on the gain that has built up since the time you bought the securities.

•*Loophole:* Be prepared to specifically identify the shares of stock you want your broker to sell. This is important when you've purchased different lots of a company's stock at different prices and you're selling less than your total holding.

If you don't tell your broker which shares you want to sell, the IRS requires you to use the first-in, first-out (FIFO) method. The shares you sell are considered the first ones you purchased. But if you can specifically identify which shares you want to sell, you can tell your broker to sell those.

Example: You can tell your broker to sell the ones you paid the most for to minimize your taxable gain on the sale. Tell him/her to sell the 200 shares of XYZ Company that you bought on October 4 for $13 a share.

Key: Keep detailed records of your purchases—the number of shares you bought, the amount you paid per share, the date of each purchase and the total dollar amount of the purchase, including such items as commissions and fees.

•*Loophole:* Swap bonds for tax losses to use against capital gains. Review your portfolio and look for bonds that have declined substantially in price since the time you bought them. Sell them and reinvest the proceeds in similar but not identical bonds—for instance, a bond of a different municipality that has the same rating as the bond you sold.

The sales will generate capital losses, which can be used to offset capital gains that you've already taken. The swap can also be used to improve your portfolio by replacing bonds that are performing badly with others that have greater income or profit potential.

•*Loophole:* Create capital losses. You may want to create losses that can be used to offset capital gains and shelter up to $3,000 of other taxable income.

As long as you are careful to avoid the wash-sale rule, you can lock in losses on securities that have dropped in value while substantially retaining your current investment position.

You can do this by doubling up—that is, buying a matching lot of the same securities as the ones you own, holding the new lot for 31 days, then selling the old one at a loss. Or you can lock in losses by selling first and buying back the same securities after waiting the required 31 days.

•*Loophole:* Deduct losses on the sale of Section 1244 stock. Only $3,000 of net capital losses are deductible each year against salary and other income. But losses on the sale of stock in a small business company (no more than $1 million of paid-in capital) may be deductible as ordinary losses far in excess of the $3,000 capital loss limitation.

The company's stock may qualify as Section 1244 stock. If it does, you can deduct up to $50,000 of ordinary losses ($100,000 on a joint return). Have your tax adviser see whether the stock is Section 1244 stock.

•Loophole: Write off worthless securities. Losses from the worthlessness of stock or other securities are deductible in the year in which the security becomes worthless. They're deductible as capital losses. One way to establish the loss is to sell the security to a friend for a nominal amount—say, a dollar.

Alternative way of establishing worthlessness: Get a letter from your broker saying that the cost of selling the security will be more than the amount realized in the sale.

Source: Edward Mendlowitz, partner, Mendlowitz Weitsen, CPAs, Two Pennsylvania Plaza, New York 10121. Mr. Mendlowitz is the author of *New Tax Traps/New Opportunities.* Boardroom Special Reports.

How to Get Money Out of a Mutual Fund...Quickly

Most mutual-fund investors don't think about getting their money out of a fund when they put it in. Too often, when financial markets dip and they want to redeem their shares, they find that getting their money back is time-consuming, frustrating and sometimes costly. *Reasons:*

•The phones are tied up. Mutual-fund offices can be so inundated with orders to buy and sell shares that their switchboards may be busy at critical times. When you call requesting information about how to redeem shares, you may have to let the telephone ring for a few minutes before someone answers.

•The procedures for redeeming shares are bureaucratic. With most funds you must not only write a redemption letter requesting a check for the value of your investment, but you must also have your signature guaranteed by a commercial bank or by your broker. That can be time consuming, especially if you bought your shares directly from the fund instead of through a broker, and you don't happen to have an account with a commercial bank. Notarized signatures aren't acceptable and most funds will refuse to accept guarantees from savings-and-loan institutions. If your personal bank is an S&L, you'll have to go to a commercial bank that your bank has established a relationship with to have your signature guaranteed.

To avoid these obstacles:

•Make a copy of the section of the fund prospectus that refers to redemption procedures —and keep it handy. That way you won't have to make a phone call to get information on redemption procedures.

•Prepare a redemption letter in advance. Have your signature guaranteed by your broker or commercial bank so you can simply date the letter whenever you decide to pull out of the fund. Follow prospectus instructions for writing a redemption letter (usually, all you need to do is request that a check be sent to your home address and give the number of shares owned and your account number).

•Consider buying shares only in stock or bond funds managed by firms that also have money-market funds to which you can switch part of or all of your account by telephone. That way you have access to the money via money-market account checks, usually within two days. *Caution:* It's always a good idea to call in a switch as early in the day as possible, because after 3 PM on heavy-volume days many fund offices can be especially busy.

•When you fill out the forms to purchase fund shares, complete the section for authorizing wire transfers of redemptions to your bank. That service allows you to have shares redeemed and the proceeds deposited directly into your checking or savings account, usually on the same day you make the request. If you need the money fast and you have trouble getting through by phone, you can request a bank transfer in a redemption letter sent by overnight mail.

Source: Sheldon Jacobs, publisher, *The No-Load Fund Investor,* Box 283, Hastings-on-Hudson, NY 10706.

How to Make the Most of Small-Cap Stocks

Stocks of smaller secondary companies can surge ahead, significantly outperforming large-company stocks.

Strategy: Concentrate on small undervalued companies in niche markets with the potential for superior earnings growth.

Perspective

Historically, small-cap stocks perform best during, and coming out of, a recession. These small-company stocks have outperformed large-company stocks for periods lasting from two to seven years, so selected small companies should still have far to go.

But success in the small-cap area will not be determined by size alone. Because of their recent run-up in prices, secondary stocks are neither cheap...nor expensive. Nor do they offer unparalleled opportunity across the board.

Rather, their future performance is likely to be much more in line with that of the market in general. Only those companies with low relative market values and the potential for superior earnings growth are apt to outperform the market during the coming decade.

Tricky Times

In the coming years, large companies will be scrambling to exploit new markets. They'll be unwilling to relinquish these opportunities to smaller companies. And if large companies resort to price wars to gain market share, the impact could be devastating for their smaller competitors.

Furthermore, large companies have a strong advantage operating and raising capital overseas, where much of US firms' future growth will come from.

Good news: Smaller companies are not burdened by the huge debt that many large companies took on during the restructuring binge of the 1980s. As a result, they are much more flexible than their larger counterparts. Savvy investors who concentrate on the basics should be able to find some standouts.

Strategy: Look for companies with a strong franchise that can protect them from competitive threats. Those companies with a niche in the marketplace, with patent protection or with a unique product that can command premium prices are those most likely to be able to turn in strong earnings growth.

Source: Mary Farrell, strategist with a special interest in small-company stocks for PaineWebber and a frequent panelist on *Wall Street Week* with Louis Rukeyser.

Dollar Cost Averaging...PLUS

Dollar cost averaging plus (DCAP) assumes the general trend of fund prices is up, but there will be price fluctuations along the way that provide investment opportunities.

How it works: You invest monthly, picking an average target for the fund's price per share. For every 5% below your target, you increase that month's investment 20%, to a maximum of 100%. If the fund's value climbs again, you reduce the additional investment 20% for each 5% increase, until you return to your original base-line investment.

Source: *Mutual Funds: Your Key to Sound Financial Planning* by Lyle Allen, former member of President Nixon's Wage and Price Control Board, now retired in Logan, VT. Avon Books.

CD Savvy

Many brokerages offer certificates of deposit that pay higher interest than those offered at local banks. The CDs come from various banks throughout the US. All are federally insured up to the $100,000 limit. And—there is no commission charged.

Source: Lewis J. Altfest, L.J. Altfest & Co., a fee-only financial planning firm, 140 William St., New York 10038. He is author of *Lew Altfest Answers Almost All Your Questions About Money.* McGraw-Hill.

CHAPTER THREE
Tax Savvy

Great IRA News from the IRS

The IRS has announced dramatic changes in the rules for IRAs. These changes correct almost every mistake people can make with them. *Payoffs...*

•It is now much easier to maximize benefits from IRAs—making them an even better retirement saving device than before.

•Persons who made mistakes with IRAs that were irreparable under old rules, and that could have cost their families large amounts of tax savings, now can get those lost savings back...and maybe even more!

The Good News

On January 11, 2001, the IRS released new Proposed Regulations for IRAs which may comprise the greatest tax simplification in history. While still in proposed form, they can apply to required distributions in 2001.

The new regulations overhaul distribution rules for IRAs—and for qualified retirement plans, such as 401(k) and 403(b) plans, as well.

And the changes are entirely pro-taxpayer!

Explaining the changes, the IRS said that the rules used until now to govern IRAs have been "unreasonably restrictive" and "too complex."

Examples it cites: The requirement that IRA beneficiaries be named by the time the IRA owner turns age 70½, even if circumstances change later...the complicated distribution-over-life-expectancy calculations for minimum annual distributions from IRAs.

The IRS realized that honest misunderstandings of the old rules, and inadvertent failures to comply with them, could be very costly to taxpayers—and says the new rules are meant to prevent such errors from occurring.

Result: Almost all the complex elections that IRA owners had to make under the old rules have been eliminated. And, under the new rules, even basic mistakes regarding beneficiaries and distributions can be corrected—even after an IRA owner dies!

Simpler

Major simplifications under the new rules...

•Distribution method. IRA owners no longer are required by age 70½ to elect the "recalcula-tion," "term certain," or "hybrid" method of calculating minimum required annual distributions to be taken over their lives.

All IRA owners and participants in 401(k) plans, etc. will use the same favorable method. Until now known as the MDIB (Minimum Distribution Incidental Benefit) method, this uses the joint life expectancy of the IRA owner and a person 10 years younger than the owner as the period over which distributions must be taken.

Key: Under the new rules this method is used even if there's no beneficiary, or the beneficiary is not 10 years younger.

Example: A 72-year-old has $100,000 in her IRA and doesn't have a named beneficiary. Under the old rules, her required minimum distribution would have been $6,849. Under the new rules, it's just $4,098.

Benefit: Most IRA owners will become entitled to take smaller minimum required annual distributions—lengthening the potential lives of their IRAs—starting right now! That's because most IRA owners don't have a beneficiary at least 10 years younger than themselves, but now are allowed to take distributions as if they do.

Exception: IRA owners who have a spouse more than 10 years younger than themselves will be able to calculate required distributions over their actual joint life expectancy —which is even better than using the MDIB method. They will be the only group not to use MDIB method.

•Beneficiary designations. IRA owners no longer have to name their IRA beneficiaries by their "required beginning date" (RBD) for taking distributions at age 70½—a key requirement under prior rules.

Since the choice of beneficiary no longer affects the size of minimum required annual distributions (which now are the same for everybody), IRA owners are free to name beneficiaries—and to change them—any time they want.

Under the new rules, the designated beneficiary whose life is used to calculate post-death distributions of the inherited IRA is not determined until December 31 of the year following the year of the IRA owner's death.

This allows for post-death planning as follows: A named IRA beneficiary can be changed after the IRA owner's death if the beneficiary "disclaims" beneficiary status in order to have the IRA pass to a contingent beneficiary.

Strategy: These new rules underscore the importance of having a beneficiary and a contingent beneficiary. Simply naming a beneficiary allows that beneficiary to spread distributions over his/her lifetime. IRA owners older than age 70½ now can change beneficiaries as family circumstances change—and select new beneficiaries, such as grandchildren, who will have the longest lives over which IRA distributions can be taken.

The total life of an IRA may be greatly extended in this way, and the tax benefits it provides to the family greatly increased as well.

Payoff

Even IRAs that have been grossly mismanaged in the past now can be "redeemed" and restored to full value.

Example: An IRA owner neglected to either elect a distribution method or name a beneficiary by his RBD at age 70½.

Under the old rules…

(1) Minimum required annual distributions were larger than necessary, so the IRA would be depleted prematurely, and…

(2) Because there was no beneficiary, the IRA would have to be liquidated soon after the owner's death—its life could not be extended.

But under the new rules…

(1) The IRA owner can't make the mistake of selecting a wrong distribution method, or of not selecting one at all. He's guaranteed the "best possible" method.

Saver: Persons now older than age 70½ who neglected to select a distribution method can use the new rule's method now—and extend their IRA's maximum life span.

(2) Even if no beneficiary was named at age 70½, one can be named at any time during your lifetime. This makes it possible to extend the life of an IRA over the lifetime of a beneficiary.

Saver: Persons already older than age 70½ who failed to name beneficiaries can now take advantage of this new rule like everyone else—curing what formerly stood to be a very costly error.

Source: Ed Slott, CPA, E. Slott & Co., 100 Merrick Rd., Ste. 200 E, Rockville Centre, New York 11570. www.irahelp.com. A practicing CPA for more than 20 years, Mr. Slott is a nationally recognized IRA distributions expert. He is publisher of *Ed Slott's IRA Advisor*, 800-663-1340.

Best Places to Retire to Taxwise

Few people decide to retire to a particular state solely because of tax reasons. Most people select a retirement community because of friendships, relatives or lifestyle—a warm climate, a slower pace, etc. But you can combine taxes and other reasons if you do a little planning.

Trap: People often forget to factor in estate taxes in thinking about a retirement state.

Minimizing Estate Tax

The best states to retire to are those that have what is known as a *pick-up tax* for estate-tax purposes. This is the lowest amount of death tax a state imposes.

Pick-up tax credit runs from 0.8% of the federal taxable estate to 16%, which is the maximum amount of credit the federal government gives for state death taxes.

The low-tax states which impose a pick-up tax are…

•Alabama, Alaska, Arizona, Arkansas, California, Colorado, District of Columbia, Florida, Georgia, Hawaii, Idaho, Illinois, Maine, Minnesota, Missouri, Nevada, New Mexico, New York, North Dakota, Oregon, Rhode Island, South Carolina, Texas, Utah, Vermont, Virginia, Washington, West Virginia, Wisconsin, Wyoming.

The Generation-Skipping Tax

Some states that have a pick-up tax impose a *generation-skipping tax*, similar but in addition to the federal generation-skipping tax. A generation-skipping tax taxes gifts and bequests that bypass a generation of heirs.

A gift that goes from a grandparent to his/her grandchild is a generation-skipping gift because it bypasses the parent's generation. The government is deprived of the tax in the parent's generation, so it taxes the original gift to make up for this.

Most states have an exemption from the generation-skipping tax for a certain amount of generation-skipping gifts. The federal exemption is $1 million. In some states the generation-skipping exemption is that high, but in others it is not.

The states that impose a generation-skipping tax are…

•Alabama, Arizona, California, Colorado, Florida, Illinois, Missouri, Nevada, Rhode Island, South Carolina, Texas, Virginia, Washington.

If you're planning to make very large gifts directly to your grandchildren, you might want to avoid a generation-skipping-tax state.

Income Tax

Some of the favorable states that impose only a pick-up tax do not have an income tax. *Those states are…*

•Alaska, Florida, Nevada, Texas, Washington, Wyoming.

Caution: Some of the states that don't impose an income tax have other taxes. *Example:* Florida, which imposes an *intangibles tax*—a tax on stock and other intangible assets.

Switching States

When you decide on a state in which you want to retire, make sure that you affirmatively change your domicile so your old state cannot come back and tax you as a resident as well. *Prudent steps…*

•Spend a greater portion of each year in your new domicile state.

•Execute and file a declaration of domicile with the appropriate office in your new domicile state.

•Dispose of your home in your old domicile state.

•Register and vote in your new domicile state.

•File all tax forms at the IRS Service Center for your new domicile state.

•Register cars, boats, etc., in your new domicile state.

•Sign a new will in your new domicile state.

•Obtain a driver's license in the new state and surrender your old license to your previous domicile state.

•File a final resident tax return in the old domicile state.

Tax Checklist

Become familiar with all of the various taxes in the state to which you are planning to move. Income tax is important, but it's not the only consideration. *Also…*

Sales tax:

•What is the rate?

•What does the state tax?

•Is there a county sales tax?

Gift tax:

•Does the state you are moving to impose a gift tax?

•What is the rate?

•Is there a minimum exempt amount?

Estate tax:

•Which assets are subject to tax?

•What is the tax rate?

•Does your state have the marital deduction?

Income tax:

•Which assets are taxed?

•How are retirement-plan distributions taxed?

•What is the tax rate?

•If there is no income tax, is there an intangibles tax?

•What is the rate of the intangibles tax?

Source: Tamara G. Telesko, vice president, manager of the financial and estate-planning departments, Chase Manhattan Bank, US Private Banking, 1211 Avenue of the Americas, New York 10036.

Summertime Tax Deductions

You'll get extra enjoyment from summer travel or a vacation home when you take advantage of opportunities to deduct their cost. *Here's how…*

Domestic Travel

By combining business with pleasure, you are able to get business deductions for a trip that has a large element of pleasure.

The basic rule for travel within the United States is that if your primary motive for making a trip is business, you can deduct the full cost of travel to and from your destination—along with the cost of lodging and 50% of the cost of meals incurred there.

This remains true even if you spend a substantial amount of time engaged in activities not related to business, such as visiting friends or relatives or going to entertainment events.

Spouse's travel break: When you bring your spouse along on a trip for nonbusiness purposes, you do not have to limit your travel deduction to half of your combined costs. You can still deduct the full cost you would have incurred traveling by yourself.

Example: You can deduct the full cost of a single hotel room even if a double room costs only a few dollars more. And you can deduct the full cost of a single airfare even if a family-fare discount obtained by traveling together gets your spouse a ticket at little extra cost.

The result is that you may be able to deduct most of your combined costs when your spouse accompanies you for pleasure purposes on a business trip.

You cannot deduct extra expenses incurred during nonbusiness side trips or during an extension of your stay for nonbusiness purposes. Unless there is a bona fide purpose for the spouse's presence, you cannot deduct the separate nonbusiness expenses of your spouse, such as those for meals, entertainment and the like.

Foreign Travel

The rules are tougher for deducting travel outside the United States. Under special rules, you can deduct all of your business-related foreign travel expenses only if...

•The trip lasts seven days or less, not counting the day you leave but counting the day you come back, or...

•You spend less than 25% of your time outside the US in nonbusiness activities, or...

•You are an employee and did not have substantial control over the trip, or...

•You can otherwise establish that a personal vacation was not a major consideration for the trip.

The percentage of time spent on business activity is figured by dividing the number of "business days" on the trip by the total number of travel days. Business days include...

•Days spent traveling directly to or from your business destination—or, if you take a side trip, the number of days it would otherwise take to get to or from your destination.

•Days on which your presence is necessary at a specific location for a business purpose, even if most of the day is spent on nonbusiness activity.

•Days on which your principal activity during working hours is business.

•Weekends and holidays that occur between business days. *Example:* You travel to Canada to work on Friday and Monday, and sightsee over the weekend. All four days are business days. If you worked only on Friday or Monday, you would have only one business day.

More Business-Travel Rules

•Conventions. Attendance at a convention for business purposes qualifies a trip as a business trip. If you go to the convention for investment, political or social purposes, you may not deduct your travel expenses.

The cost of attending a business convention held outside the United States is deductible if the meeting is directly related to the conduct of your business and it is as reasonable for the meeting to be held outside the US as in it.

•Cruise ships. If you travel to your business destination by ocean liner, your travel deduction is limited to twice the highest per diem travel allowance provided to employees in the executive branch of the federal government.

You can deduct the cost of attending a business convention on a cruise ship if the ship is registered in the US and all ports of call are located in the US or its possessions. There's a deduction limit of $2,000 per person annually.

•Charity trips. You can deduct the cost of attending a convention of a charitable organization if you attend as a chosen representative, but not if you attend simply as a member of the organization.

You can also deduct travel costs incurred while away from home performing services for a charitable organization, but only if there is no significant element of personal pleasure, recreation or vacation in such travel. This rule eliminates any deduction, for example, for working on an archaeological dig in a vacation locale.

When you travel, keep a diary that documents the amount of time spent on business or charitable activity.

Vacation Homes

The vacation homes that people enjoy during the summer can also be a source of valuable tax breaks. *Opportunities:*

•Tax-free income. If you rent your vacation home out to others for 14 days or fewer during the year, your rental income is completely tax-free. You don't even have to report it on your tax return.

•Deductible expenses. If you rent out your vacation home for 15 days or more, your rental income is taxable, but you can deduct expenses related to your rental activity. These may include home ownership costs that otherwise would not be deductible, such as depreciation, maintenance expenses, utilities and insurance. The portion of such expenses that is deductible depends on the relative amount of personal and rental use.

Example: If you rent out a house for 90 days during a year and use it 10 days yourself, you can deduct 90% of the home-related costs.

Limit: You will not be able to deduct costs that exceed your rental income if you make personal use of the house for more than the greater of 14 days or 10% of the number of days it is rented to others. Use by members of your family is counted as personal use.

If you do not exceed this personal-use limit, you can deduct up to $25,000 of net rental losses against your income from other sources (such as salary). This deduction phases out as your Adjusted Gross Income increases from $100,000 to $150,000.

•Mortgage interest. If your vacation home qualifies as a second residence, mortgage interest payments on it are fully deductible and it can be used to secure up to $100,000 of home-equity borrowing (against both your homes), which produces deductible interest.

To qualify a vacation home as a residence, you must use it yourself during the year for more than 14 days and at least 10% of the number of days you rent it out to others.

Note: A boat with living quarters can qualify as a second residence.

Source: Nadine Gordon Lee, partner in the personal tax and financial-planning departments, Ernst & Young, 277 Park Ave., New York 10172.

It's Not Too Late to Cut Last Year's Taxes

Make your contributions to your Individual Retirement Account (IRA) or self-employed retirement plan early. You'll cut your current tax bill and, at the same time, provide for your future.

IRAs

Anyone with employment or self-employment earnings (or income from alimony) can contribute up to $2,000 a year to an IRA. If you have a nonworking spouse, you can also start a spousal IRA and contribute $2,000 to his or her IRA.

Any extension of time to file your return will not extend your time to contribute to an IRA.

Contributions are fully deductible if you or your spouse are not covered by any company retirement plan (including self-employed plans).

If you are covered, contributions are fully deductible in 2001 only if your Adjusted Gross Income (AGI) is less than $53,000 (joint filers) or $33,000 (single).

They're partially deductible if your AGI is $53,000 to $63,000 (joint), $53,000 to $43,000 (single) or $10,000 or less (married filing separately).

If your AGI exceeds these limits, contributions are not deductible. You can, however, make traditional nondeductible contributions regardless of income. *Advantage:* They accumulate tax-free until they are withdrawn.

Loophole: If your company has a profit-sharing plan but doesn't contribute or allocate forfeitures to your account for a particular year, your IRA contribution for that year is deductible.

Starting the year in which you reach age 70½, you are no longer eligible to contribute to the IRA, even if you continue to work.

Loophole: If you have a nonworking spouse under age 70½, you can contribute up to $2,000 each year to a spousal IRA.

You may want to forgo an IRA deduction in favor of contributing to a nondeductible Roth IRA. Earnings in a Roth IRA are tax-free if certain conditions are met.

Starting an IRA: Experienced investors will probably want a self-directed IRA. A financial institution must be named as trustee, but you'll make the investment decisions. Prototype plans, pre-approved by the IRS, are available from the financial institution.

First, decide what investment alternative—mutual fund, CD, etc.—you wish to pursue. Then pick an appropriate financial institution based on rates, convenience, etc., and fill out the simple form for the plan you've chosen.

Self-Employed Retirement Plans

If you have self-employment income, you can set up a self-employed retirement plan—in addition to your IRA and any other retirement plans in which you participate.

You needn't run a full-time business. You qualify if you have income from consulting work, freelancing, director's fees or a sideline business.

Caution: If you have employees, you must include them in the plan (except people under 21, part-timers and those with less than a year's service). If you have more than one business or derive your self-employment income from a "related business," you generally cannot have a self-employed retirement plan just for the one business.

Note: Partnerships may set up qualified retirement plans—but individual partners are not allowed to. For instance, if you and a partner are in business together, you can set up a joint plan…but you can't each have a separate qualified retirement plan.

Contributions to the plan are tax-deductible, and you can contribute as long as you have self-employment income, regardless of your age. Limits depend on the type of plan. *There are two kinds:*

•Defined contribution plans. These are most common. They can be…

•Money-purchase plans. You commit yourself to contribute a specified percentage of self-employment income each year, to a limit of 20% or $35,000, whichever is less.

•Profit-sharing plans. You contribute whatever amount you choose each year—or nothing at all. The limit is 13.04% of self-employment income or $35,000, whichever is less.

•Combination plans. Offered by many banks and financial institutions. These allow you to contribute up to the 20% money-purchase limit, while retaining some of the flexibility of a profit-sharing plan. Ask your bank or broker.

The above limitations will be slightly lower to the extent of your deduction for self-employment taxes.

•Defined benefit plans. You set a benefit goal for retirement. You may contribute up to 100% of annual self-employment income or you may contribute the amount necessary to fund a retirement benefit of $140,000 for 2001. (The dollar limit is actuarially reduced for retirement before age 65.) You then contribute whatever is necessary to reach this goal.

It sounds complicated—and it is. You'll need professional help. But for taxpayers nearing retirement, a defined benefit plan permits much larger contributions than would be possible under a defined contribution plan.

Deadline: You can make contributions up to the due date of your tax return. An extension of time to file does extend your time to contribute. However, you can't contribute unless you had established a plan by the end of the taxable year—normally December 31.

Loophole: If you neglect to set up a qualified plan by the end of 2001, you have until the due date of your 2001 tax return to set up a Simplified Employee Pension (SEP) plan. For SEP purposes, you are considered an employee as well as employer. Contribution limits are the same as for a self-employed profit-sharing plan. If you choose, you can set up a self-employed plan later and roll over the SEP funds into your qualified plan.

Starting a self-employed retirement plan: As with IRAs, the easiest way is to sign up for a prototype, IRS-approved plan at a bank or financial institution.

You can also set up your own plan and appoint anyone you like as trustee, including yourself. Advance approval is advisable, although not required. Submit Form 5300 requesting an IRS determination letter and Form 8717 with the IRS processing fee.

Source: David A. Reed, tax partner and director of taxes, and Barbara J. Raasch, Southwest regional director of personal financial counseling, Ernst & Young, 2121 San Jacinto, Dallas 75201.

Medical Deductions for Nursing-Home Expenses

Deductions for nursing-home care fall into a gray area of the tax law. The types of expenses that can be taken as medical deductions depend on the reasons for being in the nursing home.

Guidelines:

•Fully deductible. The entire cost for nursing-home care—including meals and lodging—is deductible if a principal reason for being in the home is to receive continual medical services.

•Partly deductible. In situations where medical need is not a principal reason for being in a nursing home, expenses attributable only to medical care can be deducted.

Example: If your grandmother were in a nursing home because she was too frail to care for herself, she would not be able to deduct the cost of meals and lodging at the home. However, she could deduct the cost of any medical services received while in the home. Ask the nursing home operator to break the bills down into medical and non-medical care.

•Lump-sum payments. In some cases, a lump-sum fee is paid for lifetime care in a nursing home. The home should be able to provide you with a statement detailing the portion of the fee that will be required for the patient's future medical care, based on the nursing home's past experience. This amount is generally deductible in the year it is paid—even though it is for future medical care.

•Dependents' medical expenses. You may deduct medical expenses that you pay for your spouse or a qualifying dependent. Your parents or other relatives generally qualify as your dependents if you could claim a personal exemption for them on your tax return.

Note: The gross income test, which says that a dependent must earn less than $2,900 for 2001, does not apply when claiming a dependent's medical expenses. The person must be your dependent either at the time care was received or when the expenses were paid.

•Nature of services. Whether or not an expense is deductible is determined by the nature of the services provided, not by the qualifications or experience of the provider.

Example: Assume you broke your hip and hired domestic help. If that person also helped with your in-home physical therapy, you could claim as a medical expense the charges for the time spent on your exercises. It wouldn't matter if the provider were not a qualified medical professional, as long as the physical therapy program was for legitimate medical reasons and was prescribed by a doctor. However, the cost of having the same person do housework would not be deductible. The fact that your injury made you unable to do the housework yourself is irrelevant.

Reminder: Medical expenses are only deductible to the extent that they have not been reimbursed by insurance and exceed 7.5% of your Adjusted Gross Income.

Source: William G. Brennan, partner, Ernst & Young, CPAs, 1225 Connecticut Ave. NW, Washington, DC 20036. Mr. Brennan is the editor of the *Ernst & Young Financial Planning Reporter.*

Tax Strategies for Tough Times

Tax planning is more important than ever when times are tough. The money that can be saved in taxes is much more meaningful. *Helpful:* Withholding and estimated payments.

•Check withholding early in the year. Make sure the IRS is not getting more than is absolutely necessary. The aim should be to come out even with the IRS on April 15. Get a new W-4 form and carefully work through the calculations. Withholding allowances can be claimed for anticipated itemized deductions in addition to dependents.

•Base estimated tax payments on this year's tax—rather than last year's—if this year's income will be less than last year's. This will minimize estimated payments. To avoid penalties, estimated payments must total 90% of the tax for the current year or the prior year safe harbor: 100% of last year's tax if your Adjusted Gross Income is $150,000 or less in the prior year or a higher percentage (depending on the year) if your Adjusted Gross Income exceeds $150,000 in the prior year.

If You Can't Pay Your Taxes

•File your tax return on time—even though you can't pay the tax you owe. This way you'll avoid late-filing penalties. You will, however, be required to pay late-payment penalties plus interest on the tax you owe.

•Negotiate an installment-payment agreement with the IRS—if you can't pay your tax bill in full. If the debt is $10,000 or less and you meet certain tests, the IRS cannot refuse to give you an installment agreement. Discuss your financial situation with the IRS collection people and present them with a reasonable plan for paying off your debt.

•Make an offer in compromise—if your tax debt is so big that you won't ever be able to pay it. Under this IRS procedure, a taxpayer offers to settle the debt for less than the total amount involved. If the IRS is convinced that that's the most they'll get, they'll take the offer. In some cases they'll settle for a certain amount down and a percentage of the taxpayer's future income.

For taxpayers who are seriously strapped, an offer in compromise may be the only way to avoid bankruptcy. Sometimes the mere threat of bankruptcy will convince the IRS to accept an offer in compromise.

Hidden Money Sources

In troubled times, all sources of financing must be considered.

•Home-equity borrowing. Individuals who own a house may be able to take out a home-equity loan. There's a tax benefit in doing this—interest on up to $100,000 of home-equity borrowing is fully tax-deductible, no matter how the loan proceeds are spent.

Caution: If your income is low this year, the interest deduction may be meaningless.

•Retirement plans can be a source of cash in an emergency. The problem with taking money out of plans is that you have to pay income tax on the funds plus a 10% penalty if you're under age 59½. But for those whose income is low this year, the tax and penalty won't total that much because of the low tax bracket.

Tax-advantaged ways to tap into your retirement plans…

•Get short-term use of IRA funds. You can't borrow from an IRA, but you can get the use of the money for a very brief period. The tax law allows you to withdraw money from an IRA without tax consequences as long as you redeposit the funds into the IRA—or another one—within 60 days of taking them out. This is called an "IRA rollover." There are no restrictions on what you can do with the money. As long as you meet the 60-day recontribution deadline, you can use the money for personal purposes—tax-free and interest-free.

Limitation: You can make only one rollover a year from an IRA.

Caution: If you miss the 60-day deadline, the money you withdraw is subject to income tax …and a 10% penalty tax if you're under the age of 59½, unless you meet one of several exceptions to the penalty.

•Withdraw voluntary contributions you've made to your company's pension plan. If you put after-tax money into the plan, you can take it out and most of it will be non-taxable. You will, however, pay income tax on that portion of the withdrawal that represents the interest income your money has earned while in the plan. You'll also have to pay a 10% penalty tax on the income portion if you're under age 59½.

•Terminate your self-employed retirement plan and roll the money over into an IRA. You must deposit the funds from the plan into an IRA within 60 days of receiving them or you'll pay income tax and penalties on the funds. But you'll have the use of the money tax-free and interest-free for 60 days. Once you set up the IRA you could do an IRA-to-IRA rollover and get the use of the money for another 60 days.

•Borrow from your 401(k) plan. Most 401(k)s and pension plans permit borrowing. The tax law limits the amount you can borrow to the greater of $10,000—or one-half of your account balance, with a maximum of $50,000. (If you have a balance of $150,000, you can only borrow $50,000. If your balance is $10,000, you can borrow $10,000.)

Drawbacks: Interest you pay on the borrowed money is not usually deductible, regardless of how you use the money. If you leave your job with a 401(k) loan outstanding, you may have to repay it immediately or the IRS will treat the loan as a distribution. This means you will have to pay taxes on the amount of the distribution as well as possibly be subject to the 10% early withdrawal penalty if you're under age 59½.

•Take a hardship distribution from your 401(k) plan. Employees can take money out of many 401(k) plans in the case of hardship. This is defined in the tax law as "immediate and heavy financial need." The rules are very strict —but vary from plan to plan. Usual needs that justify a hardship withdrawal are medical expenses, college tuition, and payments to a bank to prevent foreclosure on a mortgage.

Problem: Hardship withdrawals are subject to tax and to the 10% early withdrawal penalty if you're under age 59½.

•Roll over 401(k) money into an IRA. If you lose your job, you can take the money that's in your 401(k) plan. You can keep the money and pay tax on it (plus the early distribution penalty) or roll it over into an IRA within 60 days, in which case you'll avoid tax and penalties. Or, you may wish to keep some of the money and pay tax on it and roll the balance over into an IRA. In either case, you'll have the use of the full amount of the 401(k) distribution for 60 days.

Bankruptcy and Taxes

The general rule is tax debts aren't wiped out by filing for bankruptcy.

Exception: Unpaid tax on returns that have a due date, or extended due date, that is more than three years prior to the bankruptcy filing can be discharged. This three-year rule is less beneficial than it might seem, however.

Exceptions to the exception: If a tax debt is still under dispute within the IRS or in the courts, it doesn't get discharged in bankruptcy even though the return is more than three years old.

And if the taxpayer has given the IRS a waiver of the statute of limitations on assessing tax, the debt isn't discharged even though three years have passed since the return was due.

Chapter 13: Tax debts may be discharged in whole or in part if the bankruptcy filing is under Chapter 13 of the Bankruptcy Code. This is for those wage earners who have steep liabilities and no assets. Generally, the court works out a payment plan by directing that a percentage of the taxpayer's salary go to creditors—and the IRS is one of the creditors. To the extent that the liabilities are greater than what the payment plan can ever pay off, they are discharged.

Limitation: Chapter 13 cannot be used where the liabilities are very substantial. To use Chapter 13, an individual must have a regular income— and owe less than $100,000 of unsecured debts and less than $350,000 of secured debts.

Source: Michael F. Klein, Jr., senior tax partner, national director of tax consulting services, Price Waterhouse, 1251 Avenue of the Americas, New York 10020.

Sideline Business or Hobby?

A favorite technique of tax auditors is to disallow a deduction claimed for a sideline business on the grounds that the activity is really just a hobby. The auditors try to establish their case by asking the taxpayer for copies of returns for the past four or five years. If the activity has produced a loss each year, the auditor will summarily conclude that the current loss is a nondeductible loss.

Helpful: Avoid falling into this trap by not taking copies of previous years' tax returns to the audit. The taxpayer, in general, has no obligation to provide copies of returns that have already been filed with the IRS. *Also helpful:* Ask the auditor where in the law it says that you must actually show a profit on a sideline business—ever. All that's required is that you intend to make a profit.

Motheraid

A son paid his mother's medical expenses with money he withdrew from her bank account under a power of attorney. The IRS disallowed the son's deduction for these expenses, saying the money was really the mother's. But the Court of Appeals allowed the deduction. The money was legally his—a gift from his mother to him.

Source: *John M. Ruch*, CA-5, 82-4463.

Future Income to Grandchildren— No Taxes Now

"Grandfather trust" is a term used to describe a trust set up by an individual for the benefit of someone he is not legally obligated to support, even though the income is, in fact, used for support purposes. Thus, when a trust's income is used to provide support for a grantor's grandchild, whom he is not legally obliged to support, trust income is not taxed to the grantor.

The trust principal would not be included in the grandfather's estate when he dies, so his tax situation benefits from such an arrangement in another respect.

The grandchild also benefits, receiving support he otherwise might not receive. And so does the grantor's son, who has been relieved of the obligation of providing support for his child.

If an individual sets up a trust with a third party, such as a bank serving as trustee, and the trustee has the authority in its sole discretion to use trust income for the support of a person that the grantor must support, such as his wife or minor child, the grantor is not regarded as the owner of the trust fund.

Source: *Estate Planning: The New Golden Opportunities* by the late Robert S. Holzman. Boardroom Classics. Out of print.

Private Foundations Are a Plus

Private foundations make sense for entrepreneurs who have sold a business or otherwise have an unusually large amount of taxable income. Immediate tax deductions can be taken up to a limit of 30% of Adjusted Gross Income, and the excess can be carried forward for five years. The founder can maintain absolute control over the foundation's operations. *Caution:* At least 5% of total assets must be given to charities or charitable activities each year. And there's a 2% federal excise tax on the net investment income of the foundation.

Source: *Legacies*, Baylor University, Box 98011, Waco, TX 76798.

IRA Trap

Don't have your IRA invest in tax-exempt state or municipal bonds. *Why:* Any amount withdrawn from an IRA is taxable income, even if the withdrawn amount was earned from a tax-exempt bond. So, by having the IRA invest in tax-exempt bonds, you forfeit the tax exemption for them that would have been available had they been held outside the IRA.

Joint/Separate Returns

Married couples can file a joint return or separate returns. Usually, a joint return works out better, especially if one spouse has appreciably higher income than the other.

Nevertheless, filing separately can be advantageous in some situations:

•Deductions for casualty losses must be reduced by 10% of Adjusted Gross Income (AGI). On a joint return, combined AGI is reduced even if only one spouse suffered the loss. If separate returns are filed, the loss is reduced by only 10% of that spouse's income.

Example: A husband has AGI of $70,000; his wife, $20,000. The wife's jewelry, worth $25,000, is stolen. On a joint return, the loss must be reduced by $9,000 (10% of combined income); on a separate return, by only $2,000 (10% of wife's income).

•The same considerations apply if one spouse, but not the other, has heavy medical expenses, since you can deduct only expenses in excess of 7.5% of AGI—or heavy miscellaneous expenses, which can only be deducted to the extent they exceed 2% of AGI.

Other options: If married persons live apart for the entire year, either spouse may file as head-of-household (with reduced rates) if he or she has an unmarried child or dependent living with him or her for the entire year. The other spouse would then have to file separately (higher rates) unless that spouse also had a child or dependent in his or her household. *Or:* They could file jointly, if that works out better.

Caution: The only way to tell for sure whether it's better to file jointly or separately is to take pencil and paper and figure the tax both ways.

Source: Mahoney, Cohen & Co., 111 W. 40 St., New York 10018.

Benefits Loopholes

Here are some ways to get the most mileage from the noncash benefits your company provides.

•Pension and profit-sharing plans. Your employer contributes money on your behalf and the money accumulates on a tax-deferred basis. You don't pay tax on the money until you withdraw it. These are the basic tax advantages, but there's more…

Loophole: Take a tax-free loan from the pension or profit-sharing plan. You can do this if the plan permits borrowing—not all do. Plans that allow borrowing usually make it easy on the participant—no need to justify why the loan is needed.

Tax-law limits: The amount you can borrow is limited to your vested balance up to the greater of $10,000 or one half of your vested account balance, with a maximum of $50,000.

Loophole: Put some of your own money into the plan—many plans allow employees to make voluntary contributions. Such contributions are not tax-deductible, but the money accumulates income on a tax-deferred basis.

Loophole: If your company's plan is inactive, in that no additions are being made and no benefits are accruing on your behalf, you are eligible to contribute to a traditional IRA.

•**401(k) plans.** You contribute part of your salary to a company-sponsored savings program. You pay no income tax on the dollars you contribute until they're withdrawn. Interest, dividends and other earnings accumulate tax-deferred until you take them out.

Loophole: Though the amount you can contribute each year is limited by the tax law, it's far more than you could put into an IRA. *Maximum 401(k) contribution for 2001: $10,500.*

•**Company-paid life insurance.** As long as the coverage doesn't exceed $50,000, you are not taxed on the premiums the employer pays. But if it is more than $50,000, you are taxed on part of the premiums.

Loophole: The taxable amount is figured from IRS tables and is less than the actual premiums the employer pays. You pay some tax for the extra coverage, but it is far less than it would cost you to buy similar life-insurance coverage outside the company.

•**Medical and disability insurance.** Company-paid insurance is not taxable to the employee.

Loophole: Even if the employee's dependents are covered by the insurance, the employee does not have to pay tax on the premiums.

Drawback: Disability payments received are taxable income to the employee.

•**Cafeteria plans** allow employees to choose between cash and a shopping list of benefits, including group medical insurance, disability, child care and the like. The employees choose their own menu of benefits. The benefits do not have to be included in the employee's taxable income.

Loophole: These plans are very easy to set up and administer.

•**Employee loans.** Employers can make interest-free loans of up to $10,000 to their employees. The employee does not have to report the foregone interest as taxable income.

•**Use of an apartment by an employee.** This is taxable to the employee at fair market rent.

Loophole: Fair market rent for this purpose is a price that is consistent with the apartment's value to the employee. If an employer puts an employee up in a three-bedroom apartment, but the employee only needs a one-bedroom apartment, the employee would only have to pay tax on the value of a one-bedroom apartment.

•**Stock with cash in tandem.** If a company gives stock to an employee as an incentive or bonus, the fair market value of the stock is taxable to the employee in the year it is received. The tax cuts deeply into the true value of the bonus. But the company gets a tax deduction for the stock's full value.

Loophole: In addition to the stock, the company gives the employee cash to cover his tax liability on the stock and the cash together. Assuming the company and the employee are in roughly the same tax bracket, the transaction will be a wash. The amount the company saves in taxes will be about equal to the amount the employee owes.

•**Incentive stock options.** When a company gives an employee what are known as "nonqualified stock options," the employee must pay tax when he exercises the options. But if the company gives "incentive stock options," tax does not have to be paid until the employee sells the stock. No taxable income is recognized by the employee when the option is granted or exercised.

Trap: The difference between the option price and the fair market value at the time an incentive stock option is exercised must be included in calculations for the Alternative Minimum Tax. It's complicated, so look into it with your tax adviser.

Loophole: The employee can, if he chooses, elect to pay tax on the value of the stock in the year that he gets the stock, not in the year it becomes available to sell. This is an election made under Section 83(b) of the Tax Code. In many instances, if the company is expected to grow very rapidly, it would be advantageous to make this election.

•**Phantom stock,** also called "stock appreciation rights," are sometimes issued to employees. No actual stock is given, but payments are made as if actual stock had been issued. If any dividends are paid to stockholders, they are also paid to the phantom stockholders. This money is taxed as compensation, rather than as dividends.

Loophole: The employee doesn't pay tax until there is an actual payment to him as a phantom stockholder. No tax is payable when he first receives the phantom stock.

•Secular trusts. These trusts have been developed to ensure that companies pay employees the deferred compensation that has been promised them. *How they work:*

The company puts money into an irrevocable trust for the employee and gets an immediate deduction for the contributions. The employee is taxed currently on all contributions credited to the trust. But, the company makes a payment to the employee to cover his tax liability. When benefits are eventually paid, the employee gets them tax-free.

Loophole: A secular trust is less expensive for a company to establish than its relative, the Rabbi trust.

Source: Edward Mendlowitz, partner, Mendlowitz Weitsen, CPAs, Two Pennsylvania Plaza, New York 10121. He is author of several books, including *Aggressive Tax Strategies.* Macmillan Publishing Company.

How to Cut Taxes on Retirement-Plan Payouts... With a Sub-Trust

Most professionals, key executives and company owners put away as much as possible in retirement plans to reap the tax savings. But putting too much into a retirement plan can backfire and siphon away up to 80% of your retirement-plan wealth.

Problem: Every dollar is subject to income tax and may be subject to estate tax as well.

You can avoid much of the tax liability on a substantial part of your retirement assets by setting up a network of trusts that include a "sub-trust."

Key: Use life insurance as the funding vehicle for the trusts. *How to do it:*

•Create a sub-trust within your retirement plan. It's called a sub-trust because your retirement plan is itself a trust.

•Create another trust outside of your retirement plan—an irrevocable life-insurance trust.

Designate a trusted individual or a financial institution as the trustee of this trust—not yourself.

•Have the trustee of the sub-trust buy a life-insurance policy on your life. Name the sub-trust as the beneficiary of the life-insurance policy. Name the irrevocable life-insurance trust as the beneficiary of the sub-trust. Name your children as the beneficiaries of the life-insurance trust, with your spouse to get income from the trust assets for life.

•When you die, the life-insurance proceeds are paid first to the sub-trust. Then they are paid over to the life-insurance trust, and from there they go to your beneficiaries.

•Have the premiums on the life insurance paid out of your retirement-plan contributions.

Tax impact: Your retirement plan pays the insurance premiums out of your contributions to the plan. Thus, what you have is a tax-deductible life-insurance policy—since retirement-plan contributions, within certain limits, are tax-deductible. *Impact:*

•Income tax is avoided because life-insurance proceeds, payable on your death, aren't subject to income tax.

•Estate taxes are avoided because neither the sub-trust nor the irrevocable life-insurance trust are part of your estate.

Rich example: By adding a $1 million insurance policy, plus these trusts, to a $1 million retirement plan, your beneficiaries will get $1.5 million instead of $500,000 after taxes. The trust arrangement triples your beneficiaries' after-tax return.

Watch out: Skilled drafting of the sub-trust and the life-insurance trust is imperative. So is fine-tuning the mechanics of the transaction, including paying the insurance premiums from the retirement plan.

The IRS has allowed sub-trusts without challenge so far. However, the technique has not yet withstood a challenge in court. But even if the sub-trust was disallowed by a judge, you would be no worse off taxwise than you would otherwise be.

Source: Alan Nadolna, president, Associates in Financial Planning, 100 S. Wacker Dr., Suite 1650, Chicago 60606.

CHAPTER FOUR

Estate Planning Strategies

Who Is the Spendthrift?

A grantor may not be concerned so much that his son or daughter has spendthrift tendencies, but that this person's spouse is the one who is likely to be wildly extravagant or gullible. The grantor may provide that anything he gives or leaves to his son or daughter is to be in the form of a life income from a trust, so that the principal cannot get into the hands of the spouse. The remainderman or remaindermen will be specified as the grantor sees fit—often the grandchildren are named, rather than the prodigal spouse.

How to Avoid the Naming Of an Administrator

To ensure that an executor of your selection will serve, this is what you should do:

1. Sound out your designated executor to see whether he will actually serve if named in your will. Do this periodically. Is his health still satisfactory? Has he taken on full-time responsibilities elsewhere? Is he still interested in you and your beneficiaries? If not, replace him.

2. Seek to ensure your designated executor's agreement to serve by recommending to him knowledgeable and able attorneys, accountants and (where appropriate) appraisers and brokers who can help him to carry out his responsibilities without excessive detail work with which he isn't familiar.

3. Name one or more successor or contingent executors, so that if the person of your choice doesn't serve, at least it will be your second or third choice, rather than an administrator that you would never have engaged.

4. Name a trust company as co-executor. This virtually assures the permanence and continuity of an executor you have seen fit to name.

5. Make certain that your will is valid so that the executor chosen by you will qualify. Have an attorney familiar with state law check such requirements as the minimum number of witnesses required. State laws vary as to the technicalities to be met.

6. Be sure that your will can be found when the time comes to have it probated. A perfectly executed and technically correct will is useless if nobody knows where it is. Have your will in your attorney's office or with your federal income-tax workpapers.

Source: *Encyclopedia of Estate Planning* by John J. Tuozzolo. Boardroom Classics.

Pass Your IRA on to Your Heirs

Most people leave their Individual Retirement Accounts (IRAs) to their spouse. But if your spouse is adequately provided for, you may want to leave some or all of your IRA money to your children or grandchildren. You get the greatest mileage from an IRA that you leave to your grandchildren or other beneficiaries who are much younger than you. *Benefits of leaving an IRA to a grandchild…*

•The IRA will continue for a long period of time—50, 60 or even 70 years, depending on the grandchild's age.

•IRA earnings will accumulate on a tax-deferred basis for that period of time. This can add hundreds of thousands of dollars to an IRA.

•There's a substantial income-tax saving in leaving money to a low-bracket grandchild rather than to a spouse. A spouse will pay income tax on IRA payouts at the 31% rate or more. But once a grandchild reaches age 14, income is taxed at his/her rate, not the parents'.

•There's an estate-tax saving. The IRA assets and their growth over the years will not be included in your spouse's estate.

•The IRA assets avoid probate.

Caution: The most you can give to your grandchildren without any generation-skipping tax is $1 million (adjusted for inflation). After that, gifts to grandchildren are subject to the generation-skipping tax, which is a 55% tax on gifts that pass over a generation of heirs—usually the parents' generation.

Problem: Few professionals know how to keep an IRA alive for a person's grandchildren. Some consultants may advise nonspouse beneficiaries to take all the money and pay tax on it the year after the account holder dies.

Solution: Understand how IRA distribution rules work. Do the paperwork now to keep the IRA alive long after you are gone.

Distribution Rules

IRA owners are required to begin taking money out of their traditional IRAs by April 1 of the year after they reach age 70½. But the distribution rules for beneficiaries are different.

•If you die before reaching your required beginning date, which is April 1 after the calendar year in which you attain age 70½, and you've named a grandchild as beneficiary, your grandchild has two options…

•*Option 1:* Take all the money in the account by the end of the year following the year of your death, or

•*Option 2:* Begin taking annual distributions based on his/her life expectancy in the year following your death. *Example:* A grandchild who was 20 at this time would have a life expectancy of 61.9 years. To satisfy the minimum distribution rules for IRAs, he/she would have to take only ⅟₆₁.₉ out of the IRA in the first year. If there was $200,000 in the IRA at the end of the year in which you died, the required distribution would be $3,231 (⅟₆₁.₉ of $200,000). The IRA would continue for another 60 years.

To use the life expectancy method (option 2), your grandchild or his trustee may have to file a written election with the IRA institution by no later than December 31 of the year after the year you die, saying the IRA money is to be paid out over the grandchild's life expectancy—61 years in the above example. Payments from the IRA must commence no later than December 31 of the year after you die.

If distributions under option 2 don't start on time, your grandchild will default into option 1, and all the money in the IRA will have to be paid out to your grandchild five years after your death.

•If you reach your required beginning date, the rules are different. You must begin taking money from the IRA by April 1 of the year following the year you reach 70½. The amount you withdraw each year can be based on the joint life expectancy of you and your beneficiary.

Example: You are 71 and your grandchild, your beneficiary, is 12 in the year you attain age 70½. (If you are born in the first half of the year, you are 70 instead of 71.) Your joint life expectancy under the IRS table is 25.3 years.

Example: You die at 74 after taking out four annual payments. Your grandchild would be able to withdraw the remaining money over his remaining single life expectancy of 65.8 years (for the year following the year of death).

Trust Required

If your grandchild is a minor, you'll need a trust for the benefit of your grandchild to handle the money being paid from the IRA. You can name a family member as trustee.

Bank accounts: On the death of the grandfather, the trustee would open up a bank account in the name of the trust. He/she would also open a custodial account for the grandchild at a bank or brokerage firm.

The trust says that money goes from the IRA to the trust, and then from the trust to the custodial account, until the grandchild reaches the age of majority—18 or 21, depending on state law. After your grandchild turns 21, the money goes directly to him. Under appropriate circumstances, the custodian could use the money to pay your grandchild's college expenses.

There's no tax to the trust because the money is going right out—the trust is just a conduit. The money is taxed to the grandchild, but at the grandchild's tax rates.

One of the advantages of having a trust is that the assets will be protected from the child's creditors, should the child have an accident or become involved in other legal problems—such as bankruptcy, divorce, etc.

Note: Even if an irrevocable trust is used, you can still change IRA beneficiaries if circumstances dictate a change. You can make IRA beneficiary substitutions until you die.

Best: A separate trust for each grandchild to whom you leave IRA money. *Cost:* About $3,500 to set up the trust (or multiple trusts for a number of grandchildren) and an annual fee of $200 or $300 to prepare and file tax returns for the trust after you die.

Practical use: This is a good way to develop a college fund for a grandchild at low tax cost.

Source: Seymour Goldberg, professor of law and taxation at Long Island University and senior partner in the law firm of Goldberg & Goldberg, 666 Old Country Rd., Garden City, NY 11530. Mr. Goldberg is the author of *A Professional's Guide to the IRS Distribution Rules.* Field Services, New York State Society of Certified Public Accountants.

Using Disclaimers to Save Estate Taxes

Despite the way it seems in the movies, the instructions in a person's will are not necessarily the last word on how assets are distributed.

After death, those named in the will can alter a decedent's estate plans—and save taxes—by filing what is known as a disclaimer.

A disclaimer is a legal document in which a person refuses to accept some or all of the benefits that result from a decedent's death.

The heir making the disclaimer cannot say who will inherit in his/her place. Under the terms of the will, the property passes as if that heir had died before the decedent.

Example: A decedent's will leaves $1 million to his adult child who is already wealthy and planning his/her own estate. The adult child does not wish to add to his estate these additional funds, so he executes a disclaimer refusing to accept the bequest. The disclaimed amount passes, as if the child had predeceased his father, to the grandchildren or other beneficiaries named in the father's will. If the disclaimer is properly executed, there will be no additional gift or estate tax.

Trap: A disclaimer must be signed within nine months of a decedent's death. Failure to act promptly can mean that the person disclaiming will be treated as making a gift, subject to gift tax, to the person who inherits as a result of the disclaimer.

Caution: Before signing a disclaimer, check to see who will inherit under the terms of the will as a result of the disclaimer. Make sure the property does not pass to someone who might not benefit from the disclaimer, such as a relative in a nursing home who is on Medicaid and can't own any property.

A disclaimer is an important after-death estate-planning tool since it is, in effect, a second chance to rework a decedent's will. This does not necessarily mean that the will is faulty. It can simply mean that since making the will, tax laws or family economic circumstances have changed.

There are certain key situations in which to consider using a disclaimer:

•To save taxes. Suppose a will provides that all property is to go directly to a surviving spouse. There will be no tax in the first estate because of the unlimited marital deduction. But the survivor's estate will be taxable. Tax in the survivor's estate could have been reduced had the decedent left $675,000 worth of property to persons other than the survivor. The survivor can, in effect, create this tax break by disclaiming up to $675,000 worth of benefits provided under the will. This $675,000 will then pass to other beneficiaries. It will be tax-exempt because of the $675,000 exemption amount every estate is entitled to. *Impact:* Less tax on the death of the surviving spouse. *Alert:* The $675,000 exemption amount will increase in increments to $1 million by 2006.

•To bring a pre-1981 will up to date. Some married couples may not have redone their wills since the laws on the marital deduction were changed way back in 1981 to allow an unlimited amount of property to pass to a spouse tax-free.

Their wills may still specify that only 50% of the estate go to the surviving spouse, with the balance in trust. That trust may provide for other beneficiaries besides the surviving spouse and would not be eligible for the marital deduction. If those other beneficiaries disclaim, it may be possible to have the trust qualify for the marital deduction. *Impact:* Less tax on the death of the first spouse.

The use of disclaimers is not necessarily limited to property passing under a will. Disclaimers can be applied to assets that pass automatically as a result of the decedent's death. For example, an individual can disclaim the inheritance of an IRA or other pension benefits.

When making a will, keep in mind the possibility of an heir disclaiming. Check that the "fall-back position," the terms that apply if the named beneficiaries are out of the picture, are conducive to disclaiming.

Example: A grandfather with successful children may not want to disinherit them. But the grandfather should be mindful of the fact that the children may choose to disclaim in order to avoid additions to their own estates. If the grandfather's will provides that bequests to minors will be distributed outright at age 18 or even 21, the children may be reluctant to disclaim for fear that their children will dissipate the property. On the other hand, if the grandfather's will provides an extensive trust arrangement for minors with distributions spread out to age 35 or 40, the children can disclaim without worry.

Source: David S. Rhine, partner and national director of family wealth planning, BDO Seidman, LLP, 330 Madison Avenue, New York 10017.

Is It Worthwhile to Avoid Probate?

It's possible to avoid probate for a good portion of your estate by establishing a living trust …or a revocable trust that directs how your assets will be managed and administered after your death.

But is a trust worth the effort?

Advantages of Trusts

•Cost savings. You may save probate fees, which in some states are a percentage of an estate's total value. You also save court costs and attorney's and accountant's fees which may be incurred in probate court.

•Privacy. Court records of probate proceedings are public. But the terms of a trust are private.

•Protection. Trusts generally are tougher to challenge than wills. Trusts aren't frozen during a probate period, so the trustee can distribute assets immediately, making it more difficult for a disgruntled heir to raise a challenge.

Drawbacks to Trusts

•You still need a will. It's unlikely you'll be able to handle all your assets through a trust. And you'll need a will to handle any unforeseen contingencies that might arise. A will is also necessary to name a guardian for your minor children.

•Cost. In addition to the cost of drawing up the trust, you'll have to pay annual trustee fees.

•Estate taxes. You do not save estate taxes by avoiding probate. Your estate-tax bill will be the same whether you use a trust or a will.

•Income tax. While you're alive, having a trust will not save you any income tax. After your death, it's beneficial to have your property pass under your will rather than through a trust. Estates, but not trusts, can pick a beneficial tax year for as long as the estate is in the administration process. Additionally, an estate can continue to deduct, for the first two years, $25,000 of real-estate passive-activity losses. A trust can't.

Source: David S. Rhine, partner and national director of family wealth planning, BDO Seidman, LLP, 330 Madison Avenue, New York 10017.

Leaving-the-Company Trap

If you take the money out of your firm's tax-sheltered 401(k), you will owe taxes on everything except the after-tax contributions.

To preserve tax benefits: Leave the money in your former firm's plans, if permitted…or transfer it to the 401(k) of your new employer…or set up a rollover IRA. *Caution:* With the IRA option, have funds transferred directly to the rollover account.

If you take the money out and personally roll it over, 20% will be withheld under IRS rules.

Source: David Ellis, editor, *Tax Hotline*, 55 Railroad Ave., Greenwich, CT 06830.

Liquidating Your Business

Distributions in excess of your original cost are subject to capital-gains tax.

Loophole: If you are near retirement, consider selling the operating assets of the business at book value, but keep the corporation intact as a personal holding company. Do not distribute the cash from the sale, but keep it in the corporation, invested in tax-exempt municipal bonds. When you die, the assets will pass to your heirs at their stepped-up, date-of-death value, and income tax on any gain will be avoided.

Source: Edward Mendlowitz, partner, Mendlowitz Weitsen, CPAs, Two Pennsylvania Plaza, New York 10121. He is author of several books, including *Aggressive Tax Strategies.* Macmillan Publishing Company.

CHAPTER FIVE

Insurance Information

Protect Yourself from Your Insurance Company

What is this world coming to? Institutions that we were taught to trust implicitly have broken their solemn promises and squandered our hard-earned money.

During the past 10 years, a number of major life insurance companies have failed, and in most cases customers with annuities or whole-life policies have been unable to withdraw the cash value of their policies.

Even when a failed insurer is on the mend, as was the case of Executive Life of California (now Aurora National Life Assurance Co.) and Mutual Benefit Life (now Anchor National Life), policyholders had few rights, and life insurance premiums were increased (dramatically, in some cases) and benefits were reduced.

During rehabilitation, the courts prohibited customers from transferring money to stronger companies, taking out policy loans, or cashing in policies until further notice.

Both eventually agreed in principle to pay about 55 cents on the dollar to policyholders who wanted their money immediately. *The new challenge:* Know what happens if your insurer fails—and what you can do now—to protect yourself.

Not at Risk

•Variable annuities and variable life policies. Policyholders with these investments at any insurer are never denied access to annuities or the full benefits of their policies as promised, even if the insurer fails.

Reason: Your money is never commingled with the general account of the life-insurance company. Instead, it is invested in separate accounts, which are not available to the insurer's creditors.

•Death benefits. It is the avowed intention of the insurer and/or its regulators and rehabilitators to pay death benefits in full.

What is at risk, however, is your access to and the eventual return of the full cash value of your policy while you're still alive.

What about State Guarantee Funds?

These are funds set up by the states to protect policyholders when life insurers fail. The terms may vary by state.

In the case of Mutual Benefit Life and Executive Life, most state guarantee funds are taking the position that they are not obligated to make up the principal losses of policyholders who accept the early settlement offers.

Example I: Colorado will pay nothing to policyholders of these insurance companies because it says they were in trouble before the state established its guarantee association in 1991.

Example II: In Minnesota, the state guarantee association agreed to make up the shortfall but won't pay out, however, until the insurance companies' final settlement, which could come in five to seven years or more.

What You Can Do

If your insurer fails, consult with your insurance agent, accountant, lawyer and/or financial planner to fully understand your options and determine the following...

•If you have taken out loans against the policy over the years, how much cash value is left in the policy?

•Will you be able to qualify for a new life-insurance policy?

•Do you still need the full insurance-policy coverage or do you need even more?

Do not pay the insurer any new money. Instead, take out an automatic premium loan from the company against the cash value of your policy. Use it to pay the interest or principal payments on policy loans and/or premium payments. In most cases it won't significantly erode your death benefits.

Executive Life or Mutual Benefit Life Policyholders: Be wary of an offer of a cash discount for cash payments. It's unlikely to be worth it. Remember, you'll only get about 55 cents on the dollar now, while it may take years before you get the full value of your policy. You are dealing with insurers that have failed to keep their promises and are financially impaired. Treat them suspiciously.

If You Are Insurable Elsewhere

If you qualify, apply for a hardship withdrawal from the failed insurer. *You may qualify if...*

•You can prove the money is needed for college tuition bills.

•You are permanently disabled or have a terminal illness.

•You have medical bills but no health insurance.

•You are being evicted from a hospital or nursing home.

That way you will get 100 cents on the dollar rather than 55 cents on the dollar for the amount you withdraw. If you win a hardship agreement, you'll receive up to $30,000 at Aurora National and up to $50,000 at Anchor National Life.

Though the criteria are extremely demanding, especially at Executive Life, thousands of hardship cases have been granted.

Call the companies for details on their policies on hardship withdrawals. Anchor National Life/800-821-7887, Aurora National Life Assurance Co./800-444-3542.

If you are denied a hardship withdrawal, take the early-settlement deal, file a claim with the state guarantee fund, hope you don't have to sue to get paid and get on with your life.

The Next Step

When you buy new insurance, investigate no-load and low-load insurance policies—as well as full-loaded insurance for the best buy. And be choosy. Buy new insurance only from strong companies rated C+ or above by Weiss Research, (800) 289-9222.

It's also important to diversify. Don't put all your eggs in what may very well turn out to be one surprisingly fragile basket. Where practical, spread your total insurance needs among a few strong companies.

If You Are Uninsurable

Review your current needs for life insurance. If they are less than they were originally, you may want to reduce the size of your insurance benefits so the money you have already paid will cover the policy.

Important: If you don't have enough cash value, do not stop making payments, which would cause your policy to lapse. While you may not have immediate access to the cash value at 100 cents on the dollar, you are still insured. Remember why you bought the policy in the first place.

Source: William E. Donoghue, publisher of *Donoghue's MONEY-LETTER* and the audiocassette service *MoneyTalk*.

Life Insurance If You Can't Pass a Physical

Can't pass the life-insurance physical? Don't give up—there may be a way.

Find an agent who knows his way with insurance companies. Their standards vary on overweight, blood pressure, smoking and other medical conditions. *Example:* Six-foot middle-aged man weighing 270—many companies would add a big surcharge premium for his age. But one company will insure him with no surcharge at all.

The agent's job is to find the exceptional company and know how to present the application in the most favorable light. Few agents do this well. You've got to insist the agent shop for you.

If an individual policy isn't available (or only at very high cost), group policies can be found in clubs, fraternal orders, religious orders, volunteer firemen. It may pay to join a club just for the group insurance. The savings on the premium is usually more than the dues.

Source: Frank J. Crisona, attorney and principal of the Crisona Agency, Box 130, Carle Place, NY 11514.

Medicare: What It Doesn't Cover

Don't fool yourself that all your old-age medical needs will be taken care of by Medicare. This program is riddled with coverage gaps. Be aware of what not to expect from Medicare.

What Is Medicare?

Medicare must be distinguished from Medicaid, which is the federal program providing medical coverage for the indigent of all ages. Most elderly people wind up on Medicaid when their assets are exhausted paying for what Medicare doesn't cover. This can be a tragedy for people who had hoped to leave something to their children.

Medicare is an insurance program for people over 65. It is subsidized by the federal government through the Social Security Administration. Each month, elderly people pay premiums to private insurance companies (Blue Cross/Blue Shield or companies like them), which act as fiscal intermediaries for Medicare. The program is overseen by a watchdog agency, Professional Standards Review Organization (PSRO), which makes sure hospitals are not used improperly. *Drawbacks:* Private insurance companies, acting in their own best interests, tend to deny benefits whenever possible. PSRO interprets Medicare regulations restrictively, since they must save government money.

Major Problems with Medicare

•Congress passed much of the Medicare legislation with the intention of helping the elderly by keeping them out of institutions. However, the local agencies administer Medicare restrictively in a misguided attempt to save money. Actually, money is being wasted by forcing the elderly into nursing homes unnecessarily. *Result:* Benefits we thought would go to the elderly simply don't materialize.

•Medicare does not deal with the problem of custodial care. It is geared toward rehabilitation, which is hardly realistic for the population it serves.

•Medicare is part of an overall supply-and-demand problem. There are simply more and more old people every year, as modern medicine enables us to live longer. While the over-65 population expands, nursing homes are filled to capacity and have long waiting lists, and Social Security benefits and services to the elderly are being cut back. *Fear for the future:* Some see the frightening possibility that euthanasia may be discussed.

Hospital Cutoffs

Hospital cutoffs are the biggest problem with Medicare today. *Example:* An elderly woman goes into the hospital with a broken hip. After surgery, she cannot go home because she can't take care of herself. She needs nursing-home rehabilitation or an around-the-clock companion at home. Because of the shortage of these long-term-care alternatives, she has to remain in the hospital, though everyone agrees she is ready to leave. But Medicare cuts off hospitalization benefits, claiming that she no longer needs hospitalization. The family gets a threatening letter from the hospital—if she isn't out in 24 hours, the family will have to pay privately. At approximately $300 per day for a hospital bed, the family's assets will be wiped out very quickly.

The Appeal Process

The only way to deal with such unfair (and inhumane) bureaucratic decisions is to appeal them aggressively. Appeal is a long and costly process, but a $300-per-day hospital bill is even more costly. Also, as good citizens, we must make our government accountable for benefits promised but not delivered.

Chances on appeal: Very good. At the highest level, Federal Court, the reversal rate on Medicare cases is extremely high.

There are four levels of appeal:

•*Reconsideration* is a paper review by a bureaucrat. You can request this when Medicare is first denied. Some 95% of reconsiderations confirm the original denial of benefits.

•An *administrative law judge* will review the case after the reconsideration is denied. You

present evidence at this hearing, and a lawyer is recommended. Some of these judges are competent and sympathetic. However, many judges fail to understand the issue.

•The *Appeals Council* in Washington is the next step. They will usually rubber-stamp the decision of the administrative law judge.

•*Federal Court* is your final crack. You do stand a good chance of winning here, because judges at the federal level are not employees of the Social Security Administration. They tend to be less sympathetic to the agency's viewpoint.

At this level, a lawyer is necessary. *Important:* No new evidence can be presented in Federal Court, so be sure all your facts are presented to the administrative law judge.

Medicare and Nursing Homes

Under the law, up to 100 days of skilled nursing care in a nursing home are to be paid for by Medicare. In fact, Medicare pays for an average of only five days, claiming that nursing homes do not provide skilled care. This is another patently unfair decision that must be appealed on an individual basis.

Beyond 100 days, you're on your own as far as nursing-home care is concerned. Medicaid will take over only after your assets are totally exhausted. At an average cost of $45,000 to more than $100,000 per year (depending on your area), few families can afford long-term nursing-home care. *Important:* Plan ahead for this possibility well before a nursing home becomes necessary. Transfer your assets to your children or set up a trust fund that the government can't invade. *Be aware:* You may be liable for payment if your assets have been transferred within three years (five years for transfer to a trust), before entering a home.

Recommended: Consultation with a specialist in elder law. Ask your lawyer or a social worker in a local hospital or nursing home to recommend one.

Home Care

The home care situation under Medicare is also dismal. Medicare will pay for a skilled person to come into the home occasionally on a doctor's orders to perform tasks such as giving injections or physical therapy. There is virtually no coverage for the kind of help most elderly people need—a housekeeper/companion to help with personal and household tasks. Many senior-citizen groups are currently lobbying for this type of home custodial care to be provided by Medicare.

Assignment rate:

As far as general healthcare is concerned, Medicare supposedly pays 80% of the "reasonable rate" for medical care as determined by a board of doctors in the community. In reality, the "reasonable rate" is usually set so low that most doctors will not accept it. So, instead of paying 20% of their doctor bills, the elderly frequently wind up paying 50% or even more. *Suggestions:*

•Don't drop your major medical insurance when you retire. If you keep it up, it will cover the gaps in your Medicare insurance. It is extremely difficult to buy such coverage after you reach 65.

•Be wary of insurance-company policies that supplement Medicare. You must be extremely careful when you buy one. Be sure it complements rather than duplicates Medicare coverage.

•Get together with other senior citizens to create consumer leverage. If a group of 50 seniors go to a doctor and all promise to patronize him providing he accepts the Medicare assigned rate, it might be worth his while.

Source: Charles Robert, an attorney specializing in elder law, Hempstead, NY.

When You Don't Need Medigap Insurance

Medigap insurance may not be needed. If you are enrolled in a health maintenance organization or competitive medical plan that has a contract with Medicare, extra coverage is not necessary. And individuals who qualify for Medicaid do not need—or qualify for—supplemental insurance.

Source: *Your Parent's Financial Security* by Barbara Weltman. John Wiley & Sons.

Social Security and You... And Your Family

The Social Security system, including Medicare, has become too complicated for anyone but an expert to understand in full.

But you can—and should—know at least your basic rights, how to protect them and how to make sure you get all the benefits you're entitled to.

Check Your Records Regularly

The Social Security Administration sends you an earnings statement about three months before your birthday. If you do not receive it, request Form 7004, Request for Earnings and Estimated Benefit Statement from any Social Security office (1-800-772-1213; www.ssa.gov/on-line /forms.html). Check your record at least once every three years.

Reason: In most cases, the statute of limitations prevents correcting the records after three years, three months and 15 days.

The Statement will also include an estimate of the benefits you'll receive if you retire at age 62, your normal retirement age, or age 70, as well as the benefits payable in the event of your disability or death. The figures are based on your earnings record and your own estimate of future earnings.

This statement is indispensable for financial planning—regardless of your age. Social Security isn't just a retirement system. It also provides benefits for survivors if you should die. Your children, for example, could receive benefits until they reach age 18 (19…if attending high school …or permanently if the child is disabled before age 22). Total family benefits could exceed $20,000 a year.

Other survivors who might qualify: Widows, widowers, grandchildren, dependent parents, divorced spouses.

When to File

It's best to file a few months before you retire, but you don't have to. Retroactive benefits can be paid for six months back from the month of filing.

Important exception: If you retire before age 65, no retroactive benefits are payable. Benefits can start no earlier than the month you file. So don't delay.

You're eligible for Medicare at age 65, even if you don't retire, so you should file at that time.

For Part A hospital insurance: You can also file at any time afterwards.

For Part B medical insurance: The rules are more complicated…

You can file during a seven-month initial enrollment period—the month you reach age 65… three months before…and three months after.

If you don't file during that time period, you can file only during general enrollment periods—January 1 to March 31 of each year. If you wait more than a year, you'll be charged an extra premium—10% higher for each 12 months delay.

Exception: If you work past age 65 and are covered by your company's health plan, there's no penalty if you wait until retirement to enroll. If you're covered by your spouse's company plan, you can enroll when your spouse retires.

Delaying Retirement

If you reached age 65 in 1993, your monthly benefit increased by $\frac{7}{24}$ of 1% for each month you delayed retirement. If you reach age 65 in later years, the increase is even greater, reaching two thirds of 1% per month in 2010.

Continuing to work can increase your benefit in another way. Benefits depend on your average monthly earnings in work covered by Social Security, figured all the way back to the 1950s. *Continuing to work can increase this average in two ways...*

•The amount of wages covered by Social Security has increased faster than inflation. In the early 1950s, only $3,600 a year was subject to Social Security tax. Even after adjusting for inflation (as the law requires), this comes to only a little over $20,000—compared with the current maximum in 2001 of $80,400.

•You're probably nearer the maximum end of the scale than you were in your younger years.

Taxation of Benefits

Up to 85% of your benefits may be taxable if your "income" exceeds $44,000 (joint returns) or $34,000 (singles) or zero if you're married filing separately. "Income" includes taxable income plus tax-exempt municipal-bond interest. Some investments, however, produce returns which do not count as income.

•Annuity payments are partly income and partly a tax-free return of your capital investments. Ginnie Mae securities also provide regular payments that are partly a tax-free return of capital. Many utility stocks pay tax-free dividends that are considered return of capital.

•US Savings bonds. Interest on Series EE or I bonds doesn't have to be reported as income until the bonds are cashed.

•Growth stocks often pay no dividends. Instead, they use the profits to expand the business. Stockholders have no taxable income until they sell the stock.

•Rental real estate often produces a positive cash flow, but no taxable income, because of deductions for depreciation. (It may even show a tax loss.)

Caution: Some of these investments (real estate, especially) may tie up your cash. Don't consider them unless you're sure you have enough to live on.

Medicare

•Long-term care. The most common—and most serious—misconception about Medicare is that it provides for long-term nursing-home care. It does not. It covers only short-term stays (up to 100 days a year) in a skilled nursing-care facility.

I would urge everyone to consider buying long-term care insurance. Look for a policy that covers custodial care as well as skilled care, does not require a prior hospital stay and provides for home care without requiring a prior nursing-home stay.

•Know your appeal rights. You can't learn all the complex Medicare rules, but you should know that you have the right to appeal from any adverse decisions. Don't hesitate to exercise this right. *Prime examples:*

•Hospital stays. If Medicare decides hospitalization is no longer necessary, you must be notified in writing. At that point, you'll either have to go home...or pay all costs if you remain in the hospital. Appeal at once.

Your Medicare coverage is automatically extended while the appeal is pending...plus 24 hours. Even if you lose, you can remain in the hospital at Medicare's expense while the appeal is processed.

You also have appeal rights from the denial of nursing-home stays or home care.

•Doctor's bills. If Medicare denies payment of a doctor's bill or does not pay what you regard as enough, don't hesitate to appeal. About 75% of such appeals have resulted in higher payment.

Source: Peter J. Strauss, Esq., partner, Fink Weinberger, PC, 420 Lexington Ave., New York 10170.

You Can Fight Insurance Companies...and Win

I hear horror stories every day from families whose insurance companies refused to make timely payments on legitimate claims. Individuals are inhumanely hounded by collection agencies because their insurance companies haven't paid the bills they are legally obligated to pay. The disabled are forced to go on welfare. Some people have even been driven to attempt suicide.

Very few people—fewer than 1% of those with insurance claims—question claim denials. By not questioning a denied claim, there's a good chance your insurance company is cheating you out of money that rightfully belongs to you.

Good news: Most of those who do challenge insurers either win their cases or significantly improve their positions.

What It Takes to Win

•Positive attitude. Don't assume "they" must be right and take the first *no* for a final answer. Insurance companies count on the fact that most people simply accept their decisions.

•Persistence. The adage, "a squeaky wheel gets the grease," is true when it comes to dealing with a claim denial.

•Knowledge. Educate yourself on specific issues and the tools available to help you fight a large insurance company.

You Be the Judge

On any claim refusal, exercise your rights as a consumer…

•Insist on a written explanation. Most state laws require an insurance company to give you one.

•Compare the explanation you get from the company with the language of the policy. Insurers notoriously write policies that are difficult to understand and then interpret them to their own advantage. But in court, where language is unclear, the meaning is construed against the insurance company. Some courts have even held that the reasonable expectation of the policyholder governs the meaning of policy language.

•Rely on your own common sense. Judge for yourself "what is fair" and "what you expected." If what the insurance company offers doesn't seem fair, there is a good chance that it isn't.

•Don't be put off if your claim is denied for technical reasons. An insurer cannot deny benefits because you filed late or filled out a form improperly unless the company can show it has been harmed by your failure. That's very, very rarely the case.

•Use intermediaries to press your claim. The agent who sold you the policy, or if you have a group policy, the administrator who handles claims for your company, can often give a decisive nudge to the insurer.

•Always put your claim in writing. Arm yourself with supporting evidence. One of the most common reasons insurers give for rejections is that a bill exceeds regular and customary charges. But some companies use outdated fee schedules or averages that don't apply to your case. Get written estimates from other doctors for the same treatment to prove your point.

Example: One woman who received much less than she expected for a Cesarean delivery called 27 doctors in her area and asked what they charged for a C-section. Only three charged less than her gynecologist, and 10 charged more. Faced with these figures, the insurer paid up.

•Pursue your claim up the company's chain of command. Keep written notes of every conversation—who you talked to, his/her telephone extension, what was said.

Go the Extra Mile

If the insurer continues to stonewall, seek outside help. *Sources:*

•States' department of insurance. Most try to identify and prevent unfair claims practices. Strong ones—like California, New York and Illinois—will even act as a referee between you and your insurance company.

•Small claims court. Sue the insurer yourself if the claim does not exceed the maximum recovery amount for small claims court, usually between $1,000 and $2,500. Rather than spending their time and money to defend themselves against you, the company may well settle.

•Lawyer. It isn't hard to find one who will work on a contingency basis if you have a really strong case. You may end up collecting not just the claim amount, but additional sums for economic loss, emotional distress and—if the company has been really unscrupulous—punitive damages for wrongful conduct.* *Example:* A client of mine had a $48 gripe against his insurance company, which refused to pay for medicine. After we proved the company had fraudulently changed its basic policy coverage, the jury awarded him $70,000 in compensatory damages—and $4.5 million in punitive damages.

Whichever routes you take, the important thing is to keep pushing to get the benefits you rightfully deserve. Don't be a victim.

*Group policyholders governed by Employee Retirement and Income Security Act (ERISA) regulations can recover only policy benefits from successful lawsuits.

Source: William M. Shernoff, a consumer-rights lawyer who practices in Claremont, CA. He is the author of *How to Make Insurance Companies Pay Your Claims and What to Do If They Don't.* Hastings House.

Mistakes When Filing Insurance Claims

•Failure to accurately calculate losses. It's hard to believe, but many people can't accurately determine their losses—whether by damage or theft. *Reason:* They fail to maintain effective accounting and record-retention procedures to document the losses. It's not uncommon to hear of a situation in which a theft loss amounted to $250,000 but the claimant could substantiate only $100,000 of the loss. It's important to plan ahead with your accountant to determine the best procedures for demonstrating what you own in case you have to make a claim.

•Overstating the loss. This is a subtle problem. If a claimant purposely overstates the loss to the point where the insurance company could question his integrity, the latter will take a hard line. Generally, if the claimant takes a fair position, the insurer will still bargain over the loss claim but will be more reasonable.

•Underestimating the loss. This sounds like a contradiction of the above, but it's not. Immediately after losses are claimed, the adjuster will ask the claimant for an estimate of the damage, not an accurate, justified number. The insurer requires such a rough estimate, but be wary of providing a number before taking the time to get a reliable estimate. If the adjuster reports a number that's too low and then must go back later to the insurer and restate it much higher, both his credibility and yours are hurt. He looks foolish. Those hurt feelings can make future loss negotiations tricky. So tell the adjuster about any problems you have in coming up with a number.

Health Insurance: How to Determine Adequate Coverage

Most of the shortcomings in medical insurance occur because buyers are unfamiliar with what is available in the market. They don't have a checklist of questions to ask. Even many brokers are unaware of the pitfalls in some policies. So read the terms of the contract before you buy. Once you have a policy, fighting for additional payments is very frustrating. Therefore, have the right policy in the first place.

Many hospitalization and surgical policies do not cover the entire cost of a hospital stay or surgery. *Example:* Many plans only cover a semiprivate room up to $200 a day. Many surgical plans, such as Blue Shield, insure operation costs on a national average basis. Therefore, if you have an operation in New York, Boston or San Francisco, you are apt to have significant out-of-pocket expenses, since doctors there charge considerably more than in, say, Kansas City.

To supplement such plans, get a major medical with a sizable deductible that "wraps around" your primary hospitalization and surgical coverage. These policies can enable you to have a private nurse or specialized care in many cases.

In areas where Blue Cross/Blue Shield is noncompetitive in price or benefits, and there is no prepaid group plan such as a Kaiser-Permanente or Health Insurance Plan (HIP), get a comprehensive major medical plan from a private insurer.

Read the terms of the insurance contract to determine what the insurance company will pay for each situation. Private insurers often use the phrase "reasonable and customary charge" to limit what they will pay for operations and doctors' services. *Reasons:* The insurer wants to discourage victims of illness from visiting very expensive specialists for any minor complaint. However, "reasonable and customary" falls within a fairly wide spectrum and is negotiable up to a point. Limitations are not absolute.

Example: A New York resident flew across the border to Montreal for a gallbladder operation. He was able to prove that the operation with the cost of the flight was cheaper in Canada than a doctor and hospital in New York. The insurance company found the case convincing and paid air fare and all bills.

However, some insurance firms establish inside limits or scheduled benefits for various operations. Each situation is described with the sum the insurance company gives for room, board and the surgery. Read these carefully. Check out how these limits compare with actual practices in your region. If possible, avoid these policies and stick to the reasonable and customary policies. Obviously, you get what you pay for. Policies with inner limits are cheaper, but the cost differential is minimal.

Look into the limits of major medical insurance. Are they lifetime or per cause limits? *How they work:* If you have a $250,000 lifetime limit and get cancer treatments that use up the $250,000, you are not able to collect money for treatments when you get a heart ailment the next year. But if you have a per cause limitation of $250,000, the insurer will pay up to the limit, $250,000, for the heart ailment after you use up $250,000 for cancer. If you get any other disease, then you can obtain still another $250,000 for treatment.

Check out the extent of coinsurance. Few companies will pay 100% of all medical treatment. They want the consumer to undertake some of the payments, partly to avoid malingering. Therefore, they make you pay 20% of the second $2,000, $5,000, $10,000, $50,000 or even an unlimited amount. The insurance company picks up the other 80%. Naturally, you want to avoid policies with large coinsurance clauses. With extensive hospitalization for a major illness, you could wind up being $10,000 or even more out of pocket. If your 80/20 coinsurance is limited to $2,000, you will only be a maximum of $400 out of pocket.

Source: Leon Sicular, president, Leon Sicular Associates, benefit consultants, 22 Sintsink Drive East, Port Washington, NY 11050.

Safest and Weakest Insurers...Now

Highest rated...

State Farm Life & Accident Asr. Co. ....IL......A+
State Farm Life Ins. Co. ....IL......A+
Country Life Ins. Co. ....IL......A+
Teachers Ins. & Annuity Asn. of Am. ....NY ....A+
Northwestern Mutual Life Ins. Co.. ....WI.....A+
American Family Life Ins. Co. ....WI.....A+
American Fidelity Asr. Co.. ....OK....A
New York Life Ins. Co. ....NY ....A
Massachusetts Mutual Life Ins. Co. ....MA ...A
Pacific Life Ins. Co. ....CA ...A

Lowest Rated...

National Heritage Ins. Co. ....TX ....E
Health Insurance Plan of Greater NY ....NY ....D-
Aurora National Life Asr. Co. ....CA.....D
Southwestern Life Ins. Co. ....TX.....D+
United Fidelity Life Ins. Co. ....TX.....D+
Hannover Life Reassur. Co. of America ...FL .....D+
Conseco Direct Life Ins. Co. ....PA.....D+
Security Life and Trust Ins. Co. ....TX.....D+
Savings Bank Life Ins. Co. ....CT.....D+
American Skandia Life Asr. Corp. ....CT.....D+

Source: Martin Weiss, founder of Weiss Ratings Inc., 476 Burns Rd., Palm Beach Gardens, FL 33410. Weiss Ratings Inc. rates over 20,000 financial institutions for financial stability. The firm provides safety ratings over the phone for a fee. 800-289-9222. Last update: 3rd quarter 2000.

Disability Insurance Confidential

When disability strikes, you have to replace your income with something or face losing your house, your lifestyle, savings and investments. Ironically, most people routinely buy life insurance to protect their families in case they die, but they neglect to buy disability insurance. *Fact:* Chances of being disabled during your working years are four to five times greater than chances of dying during the same period.

Comparing Policies

• *Concern #1:* How the policy defines disability. You want the broadest definition you can find and/or afford. Some policies, for example, define disability as inability to perform any of the duties required by your occupation. *Be careful:* Under many definitions, including that of Social Security, disability is the inability to perform any occupation. Under that definition, you get no payment as long as you can work at something, even if the job you can perform after being disabled is low paying.

A split definition of disability that's often used: Strict for a specific period of time and broad for the duration of the benefit period.

• *Concern #2:* The length of the benefit period. Will the policy continue to pay you after age 65? Many policies stop paying then and you may still need funds. Unless another retirement fund kicks in, you'd have an income gap.

Also: Check the waiting period, the time between the start of the disability and the actual beginning of payment of benefits. If you can wait 90 days before you need income, the premiums will be significantly lower than if you wait only 30 days.

Example: A person who is 45 years old wants a disability policy that will protect his income of $55,000 a year. Yearly premiums with a 30-day waiting period will cost $1,900—with a 60-day wait, $1,700—and for a 90-day waiting period, $1,550.

Source: Karen P. Schaeffer, Schaeffer Financial, Greenbelt, MD.

The New Problem...Aged Parents Needing Very Expensive Care

There's nothing underhanded about making an effort to conserve aging parents' assets to pass along to children, while using Medicaid to pick up much of the cost of home care or nursing-home care.

The key legal device to conserve an elderly parent's assets is the Medicaid Qualifying Trust. The parents divest their assets into the trust and receive annual interest payments. Those interest payments are then used to meet the bills of home and nursing-home care with Medicaid picking up qualifying expenses over that amount. The principal in the trust would remain intact, to be inherited by designated beneficiaries.

It is essential, however, to get expert legal advice on how this law works now in your particular state. Ask your local bar association to recommend lawyers who specialize in legal counseling on problems of the aged or call the National Academy of Elder Law Attorneys at 520-881-4005. Don't delay, since action must be taken years before Medicaid is needed.

Source: Lewis Kamin, partner, Cappa, Kamin and Goldberg, 244-14 Jericho Turnpike, Floral Park, NY 11001, a law firm that works with Corporate Consultations in Aging, Inc.

Whole Life Insurance

A typical whole life, or ordinary life, policy covers you for your entire life and offers a guaranteed death benefit—a fixed sum payable to your heirs when you die. Some whole life policies pay dividends, which can:

•Reduce your premiums.

•Buy paid-up additions to your life insurance policy to increase your death benefit.

•Be returned to you in cash.

•Be deposited with the insurance company, where it will earn interest and serve as an additional savings account.

When you purchase a whole life policy, part of the premium pays the actual cost of the insurance risk, part pays the insurer's expenses and part goes into a reserve fund known as cash value.

This cash value, which allows the premiums to remain level during your lifetime, builds up annually and grows in value on a tax-deferred basis. Insurance companies are not obligated to tell you how your premium dollar is divided.

Because of the conservative nature of life insurance, various state regulations and the desire of insurers to fulfill their obligations, these guarantees are very low. But your actual cash available is usually higher than that which is guaranteed in the policy, if your dividends are used to purchase more insurance or are left in savings accounts with the company.

The most widely used whole life contract insures one life and pays a death benefit to the beneficiary upon his/her death. A newer variation is called second-to-die insurance, which insures two lives and pays the death benefit when the second person dies. The cost of a second-to-die policy is lower than that of two individual policies.

Whole Life Drawback I: The premiums for a whole life policy are higher than those for a term policy because some of the money goes toward cash value.

Whole Life Drawback II: Not all whole life policies pay dividends. And even when dividends are paid, they are not guaranteed...but rather reflect the insurance company's earnings, net of expenses.

Ideal candidates: Individuals with estates of more than $675,000, or couples with a combined estate of more than $1.35 million in 2001, who will be hit with estate taxes upon the death of the surviving spouse.

Alert: The exemption amount for individuals will increase in increments to $1 million by 2006.

Source: Virginia Applegarth, president of Applegarth Advisory Group Inc., a Boston-based fee-only financial insurance advisory firm. She is author of *How to Protect Your Family with Insurance.* Lee Simmons Associates, Inc.

Renters Insurance Is a Must

Renters insurance protects your personal possessions in case of damage. It also covers your liability for damages that you, family members and pets inflict on other people in your rented apartment.

Renters insurance is also important because the landlord's insurance will not likely cover the contents of your apartment.

Types of renters insurance: Replacement value, which will cover the full cost to replace a destroyed item...actual cash value, a less-costly policy that repays only the actual cost of a lost item minus depreciation.

Caution: Valuable items, such as heirloom jewelry, may need separate, additional coverage.

Source: Jayna Neagle, Insurance Information Institute, 110 William St., New York 10038.

CHAPTER SIX

A Healthier You

Why You Should Brush Your Gums

Brushing the gums with a soft toothbrush can help reduce inflammation from wearing full dentures. *Best method:* Circular brushing for two-and-a-half minutes twice a day.

Source: *Special Care in Dentistry.* American Dental Association, Chicago.

Tip for Denture Wearers

Removing dentures at night can lead to aching jaws, headaches and insomnia. *Reason:* Jaws adapt to closing over teeth. If you sleep without your dentures, you may "overclose"—which strains the jaw joint and muscles. *Recommended:* If you have morning-after pain, try leaving dentures in at night (but remove them for four hours during the day).

Source: An Army study of 200 denture wearers, cited in *American Health*, New York.

You and Your Brain— Your Brain and You

We've all been taught to take care of our bodies so we can live longer, healthier lives. But mere physical survival does not guarantee quality of life. A meaningful life requires the use of a healthy brain.

Although today's Americans live longer than ever, we fill nursing homes at a record rate. *Reason:* It's not loss of physical function that conscripts most people to a nursing home...it's the loss of mental faculties.

Good news: Barring severe injury or progressive disease—Alzheimer's, Parkinson's, etc.—much loss of brain function is preventable.

Aging and the Brain

Failing brain function is not normal. It is a sign of disease, injury or neglect.

Although we lose brain cells as we age, maturing brains compensate for cell loss in ways that increase brain function.

How: The sheath around the nerve fibers grows thicker, improving the transmission of electrical signals in the brain. And the nerve fibers, or dendrites, grow new branches.

Result: More interconnections for richer, deeper thinking.

Certain kinds of intelligence, however, do decline as we age.

Example: People slowly lose their ability to work out complex problems in theoretical mathematics...although their ability to do simple calculations isn't impaired.

Applied skills—law, medicine, engineering, architecture, etc.—do not deteriorate with age. And areas that depend on interpretation—art, music, drama, etc.—are actually enhanced as wisdom and judgment deepen. The ability to speak and write also improves from age 50 to 70. And philosophers don't hit their stride until they reach 70 or 80.

Preventable Brain Drains

For every patient I see with Alzheimer's or another serious brain disorder, I see 20 who are impaired by something that is preventable or treatable. *Common culprits:*

•Depression. The number-one reversible cause of memory loss in the elderly.

People who are depressed enough to warrant professional attention suffer from reduced attention span and poor concentration. *Result:* Impaired performance and a loss of the ability to form new memories.

In severe cases, depressed brain function lessens a person's ability to retrieve old memories. In the elderly, depression can mimic Alzheimer's disease.

• Medication. Many of the medicines that a lot of older people take—for high blood pressure, sleep disorders, anxiety, emotional problems, etc.—have side effects, some of which can impair the brain.

Older people are often overmedicated, a result of seeking relief from pain and other problems. Most do not tolerate drugs in the same doses they once did. And certain medications—which are perfectly safe on their own—can cause trouble when combined with others.

•Alcohol. The number-one brain poison in our society, it's abused by 10 million Americans. Alcohol breaks down the blood-brain barrier—a built-in defense that normally protects our brain cells from poisons that enter the bloodstream. A person who is alcohol-poisoned can suffer as much disability as a person with a stroke, tumor or brain injury. The difference is in duration, not degree.

Alcohol abusers run a 30% greater risk of suicide than the general population. *Other risks:* Memory loss, vitamin B_1 deficiency, seizures, Korsakoff's psychosis (a brain disorder with severe memory loss).

•Cocaine and other illicit drugs. Opiates, stimulants, depressants and hallucinogens all penetrate the blood-brain barrier and alter brain function. Cocaine can cause convulsions, stroke and outbursts of violence.

•Lack of stimulation. This alone can seriously depress brain function.

Example: A partially blind stroke victim spent two years in a bed positioned so her sighted side faced a blank wall. It appeared her mental faculties were failing, until she was turned to face the world. *Result:* Remarkable improvement.

An interesting, challenging environment promotes increased brain function. Lacking stimulation, brain function and development are interrupted.

•Other potential brain drains. Physical illness, including stroke, pain, stress, head injury and poor nutrition.

Build a Better Brain

Our brains improve with stimulation. We can enrich our thinking, sharpen our response time and improve our memory with simple techniques of diet and exercise.

•Diet. For optimum brain efficiency, avoid excessive salt, saturated fats and sugar. Breakfast should be the big meal of the day. Eat a full breakfast high in protein such as fish, chicken, turkey or soy products. The last meal of the day should be light, and several hours before bed.

Although many doctors do not think that vitamin/mineral supplements are necessary, I do recommend them. *Reason:* Most recommendations are based on what our body needs to avoid vitamin-deficiency–induced diseases, such as scurvy, rickets and pellagra. That's not enough to keep the brain healthy. Various studies correlate increased vitamin intake with improved verbal and non-verbal intelligence, behavior, memory and visual acuity. *Note:* Check with your doctor before you take any supplements.

•Exercise. The brain benefits from mental exercise the same way the body does from physical activity. *Suggested:*

•Balance your checkbook without using a calculator. The mathematical centers atrophy with disuse. Math exercises maintain skills and improve concentration and attention.

•Practice printing with your nondominant hand. Start by making large letters. Don't worry if they're not perfect. *Goal:* To develop speech abilities in the nondominant side of your brain. This will facilitate quicker recovery in the event of a stroke.

•Draw geometric figures and designs. You can do this while you're on the phone. Then copy the drawings with your nondominant hand. *Goal:* Improved perception of complex spatial relations and integration of both brain hemispheres.

•Put information you want to remember in a verse or song. Melody and versification are generated in the nondominant hemisphere. Combining melody with lyrics employs the whole brain and improves retrieval.

•Read challenging material. Good choices include histories, technical information, biographies, quality novels by writers with a good grasp of language (Proust, Austen, Stout, etc.). Read aloud. Listen to books on tape.

•Punctuate brain activity with brain rest. Brain rest is not the same as napping or watching TV. Brain rest requires temporarily shutting down some brain function.

Example: Sit quietly, close your eyes and progressively relax the parts of your body that use the brain most—the lips, tongue, thumbs, index fingers and big toes. Learn this exercise when you are not stressed.

•Avert inaction. Doing is more rewarding and enriching than watching. Sensory stimulation in its active rather than passive forms is terrific brain food. *Suggested:* Don't just look at art—paint...don't just listen to music—play an instrument...don't just read—write.

Source: Neurosurgeon Vernon H. Mark, MD, FACS. He is co-author, with Jeffrey P. Mark, MS, of *Brain Power*. Houghton Mifflin.

Cold Weather Fact

Women suffer in cold weather more than men. A woman's body is five times more likely than a man's to respond to cold by constricting the blood vessels of the hands and feet. When your hands and feet are cold, your whole body feels cold.

Source: Thomas L. Smith, PhD, assistant professor of orthopedic surgery, Bowman Gray School of Medicine at Wake Forest University, Winston-Salem, NC.

Mental Fitness Made Easy ...Almost

Just as it takes energy and attention to stay physically healthy, it takes time and effort for us to keep fit mentally. And, just as we've learned to exercise and watch our diets, we can learn to "think like a shrink" for optimal mental health.

What Is Mental Fitness?

Mental fitness is the ability to overcome self-pity, anger, guilt and emotional isolation in favor of self-esteem, usefulness, wonder, intimacy...and the other joyful feelings that give life meaning.

Therapists who focus on solving problems quickly use an active, systematic approach to help patients identify and resolve troubling issues and emotional problems. They are called short-term therapists. We can use their techniques in our daily lives as ongoing strategies to maintain mental fitness.

How a Therapist Thinks

An effective therapist helps the patient address the universal issues with which we all struggle...

•Dependence versus independence.

•Inappropriate attachment versus the ability to separate.

•Self-sabotage versus self-actualization.

•Chronic grief versus acceptance of loss.

•Emotional isolation versus the ability to feel one's feelings.

•Distancing versus intimacy.

All of us have developed ways to avoid examining our most troublesome behaviors and feelings. The short-term therapist takes an "observant posture" to identify the patient's defenses —the common techniques we all use to shield ourselves from painful truths about our present or past experiences.

Defenses always conceal hidden feelings. So the therapist intervenes when the patient makes a defensive statement, and pursues the defense rather than the content of the statement.

Here is a sample session, greatly condensed. A hypothetical patient, Mr. J, age 52, has been laid off from his job and is very depressed.

Therapist: How did you feel when you lost your job?

Mr. J: Well, the economy is bad, and they needed to make cut-backs, so...

Therapist...hears Mr. J rationalizing: Yes, but how did you feel?

Mr. J: Like there's nothing I can do about it. I'm too old to start again.

Therapist...challenging defense of helplessness: You're taking a helpless posture here. How did you feel?

Mr. J: Angry, lousy. After all I had done for that company!

Therapist...hears defensive anger: What was underneath the anger?

Mr. J: I felt betrayed, and foolish for having expected the company to protect me, to be loyal. And I was scared. Where would I find another job? What would happen to my family?

Therapist: Anything else?

Mr. J: I felt ashamed. I felt that I was a failure.

Therapist: What do these feelings bring to mind?

Mr. J: My father, telling me I will never amount to anything and letting me down when I needed his help.

Therapist...after further exploring the association with Mr. J's father: Were there any positive feelings the day you lost your job?

Mr. J: I felt relief, like I was suddenly free, and a strange sort of excitement that I might get to start over again doing something new.

Therapist: Anything in particular?

Mr. J: Well, I've always wanted to teach French cooking classes.

Therapist: That doesn't seem like a viable occupation now. Are you going to put your energy into proving your father right? What are you going to do about solving this problem?

By actively challenging a patient's defenses, the therapist helps him/her to recognize the underlying emotions and associations.

After this process, the therapist can then issue a call to action—What are you going to do about remedying your problem?

The "work" of therapy involves learning to take inventory of our mixed emotions. We can learn to do this on our own.

Required: A sensitivity to—and understanding of—common defenses...and unrelenting honesty.

The aim: To reach a sense of emotional balance. This lets us see our options clearly...let go of our anxiety or fear of intimacy...take action on our own behalf...change our self-defeating behaviors...and move forward.

The Defenses

Each of us favors certain defenses over others. When you notice yourself being defensive, challenge yourself to search for the emotions and associations beneath the defense. *There are three types of defenses:* Helpless, emotional and intellectual.

•The defenses of helplessness often reflect a lack of self-esteem.

•Vagueness. "I guess I feel"…"Maybe, I don't know"…"I suppose."

•Passivity and helplessness. "I can't do anything about it"…really means, "I won't do anything, I won't change."

•The emotional defenses are used to mask underlying pain.

•Crying is an appropriate response to sadness or loss. But often it masks anger, hurt or guilt. "I got so frustrated I cried."

•Depression is also an appropriate response to grief. But defensive depression usually has a self-devaluing quality, and tends to come and go. "My life is worthless."

•Anger is an appropriate response to an attack or threat. Defensive anger is a way to feel powerful and to mask feelings of hurt, insecurity, inadequacy, or powerlessness.

•The intellectual defenses are used to avoid dealing with the emotions.

•Rationalization. Explaining or making excuses to hide feelings. "She only said that because she was under a lot of stress."

•Intellectualization. Retreating into philosophy to avoid taking action. "Man was meant to be alone."

•Avoidance. Distancing from situations that are painful or intimate. Leaving the room to avoid conflict, avoiding social situations, using sarcasm to keep people away, being bossy or controlling to avoid feeling out of control.

•Denial. Denying that feelings or behaviors exist. "I wasn't drunk, the cop was a jerk. I wasn't upset at all."

•Projection. Attributing one's own unacceptable feelings or qualities to another.

Example: A man who is afraid to admit he is attracted to a woman who is not his wife says, "All these young guys want to do is chase girls."

Society's Defenses

Defenses work on a community level as well as a personal one. The more we understand how defenses work in our own lives, the better we can understand the greater issues that trouble us.

Example: Many Americans responded defensively to the Japanese accusation that American workers are lazy and illiterate, angrily Japan-bashing and smashing cars. If we were mentally fit, we would have accepted the comment in a spirit of challenge, rather than in rage. *Underlying truth:* Faced with a rather long, demoralizing recession, we have lost faith in ourselves. Our anger is a shield against the pain of believing the Japanese message.

Balance Yields Wisdom

The therapeutic process produces a growing awareness that an array of conflicting feelings usually lies beneath our defenses…that among them are positive feelings that can help balance the negative ones. ("I am angry at my father's coldness, I feel the hurt of wanting intimacy, and I also feel love and gratitude for the lessons he taught me and our moments of tenderness.")

In taking responsibility for our own contributions to our problems, we learn to stop searching for outside solutions and are no longer hostages to situations.

The quest for balance—pro and con…yin and yang—yields wisdom: Understanding of the world's complexity.

Source: Christ Zois, MD, co-author of *Think Like A Shrink: Solve Your Problems Yourself with Short-Term Therapy Techniques.* Warner Books. Dr. Zois is director of the New York Center for Short-Term Dynamic Psychotherapy, 350 E. 54 St., New York 10022.

Plastic Surgery Problems

Whether it's an ordinary nose job or the removal of a rib to achieve a smaller waistline, cosmetic surgery performed by a qualified surgeon is usually safe and effective.

As with any medical procedure, however, cosmetic surgery occasionally results in complications—in a small portion of all procedures. And when complications occur, the results can be devastating.

Cosmetic Surgery Risks

•Persistent infection. The most common complication—and usually the easiest to correct. Antibiotics are effective in most cases, although implants sometimes have to be removed.

Exception: Cartilage infections, especially those following a nose job (rhinoplasty), rarely may persist for a year or longer even with aggressive antibiotic treatment…and they can destroy the nose's shape.

Self-defense: Choose a qualified surgeon—one who has performed the same procedure dozens of times.

•Bad nose job. Nose jobs involving excessive cartilage removal can cause big trouble later in life. As the patient ages, the skin thins, and the nose appears to shrink—sometimes to little more than a tiny nubbin.

In extreme cases, a nubbin nose causes not only acute embarrassment but also breathing difficulties. The only way to correct the problem is to transplant cartilage taken from elsewhere in the body.

Self-defense: The less tissue removed during any cosmetic surgery, the safer.

•Lumpy skin. Surgeons performing liposuction must wield the cannula (fat-sucking instrument) very deftly, since uneven removal of fat results in lumpy or rippled skin. These defects are difficult or impossible to fix, even with additional liposuction or fat transplantation.

In very rare cases, fat cells liberated during liposuction cut off the supply of blood to the heart or brain. Although rare, some fat embolisms are fatal.

Also in rare cases, liposuction can result in inadvertent damage to the spleen or other internal organs. A ruptured spleen usually necessitates emergency surgery to control bleeding.

Self-defense: Use an experienced surgeon. Check out the doctor's reputation, enlist word-of-mouth recommendations and directly ask the doctor questions about his/her background.

•Barbie Doll hair. Hair transplantation is safe and effective, but the process takes months or even years to complete. Impatient patients who fail to see it through to the end often wind up with obvious plugs of hair arrayed in regular rows across the scalp.

Self-defense: Start hair transplants only if you intend to see them through.

•Distorted eyes. Surgeons performing eye tucks (blepharoplasties) must be careful to remove just the right amount of tissue around the eyes.

Otherwise, the patient may be left with eyes that seem to turn downward or outward, or with an exposed mucous membrane around the eyes.

Sometimes the eyelids are stretched so tight by surgery that the eyes cannot fully close. Botched eye jobs can also result in acute glaucoma...even blindness.

Self-defense: Choose a highly experienced surgeon.

•Lopsided face. In rare instances, face lifts damage the facial nerve. *Result:* Diminished muscle tone or even partial paralysis. The patient may develop a crooked smile, sagging cheeks or may have difficulty blinking.

Similarly, implants in the chin, cheeks and other parts of the face must be firmly attached to bone, or over time they may be mobile. More than an annoyance, mobile facial implants can result in a lopsided appearance.

Self-defense: Make sure the surgeon plans the implants so they are placed on bone.

•Rashes and redness. Collagen used to fill in acne scars and other skin defects can cause severe rashes and persistent redness. Theoretically, collagen injected directly into a blood vessel rather than just under the skin could interrupt the flow of blood to an eye—resulting in blindness.

Self-defense: The doctor should make sure the patient is not allergic to collagen before large quantities are injected. This can be done by test injections, introducing a small amount of collagen into the body in an inconspicuous place.

•Too-tight face lift. This usually occurs on repeat face lifts and strictly skin lifts. Newer face lifts include both deeper layers and skin and give a more natural look.

Self-defense: Ask what technique the surgeon uses and how much experience he/she has with the procedure. Ask to see other patients ...or their photographs.

Source: Linton A. Whitaker, MD, chief of the division of plastic surgery, the Hospital of the University of Pennsylvania, and professor of surgery, University of Pennsylvania School of Medicine. Dr. Whitaker specializes in facial surgery.

It's Important to Take Charge Of Old Age Now...

It's no longer news that more Americans are living longer—the 80-plus age group is the fastest growing segment of the US population. But for the first time, we can benefit from studies that tell us not only who is living longer, but why—and what we can do to enrich and lengthen our lives.

Recent research consistently shows that there is more to healthful aging than just staying physically fit. Maintaining strong social ties plays an essential role. And a third factor, less frequently discussed, is also important... a sense of personal purpose. *Bottom line:* People who lead purposeful lives live longer than those who do not.

Physical Health: Basic Life-Extenders

•Eliminate tobacco, regardless of your present age and health status.

•Drink alcohol in moderation, if at all. If you are one of the nation's 10 million alcoholics, get help. There are very, very few elderly alcoholics.

•Lower the amount of fat in your diet. Most Americans get up to 40% of their calories from fat. *Better:* 10% to 20%.

•Mediate the effects of stress with exercise and other techniques.

•Exercise for a half-hour daily, five days a week. Choose a solid cardiopulmonary program. Fast walking is inexpensive and effective.

Caution: Golf is not recommended. It is useless as exercise and can be stressful if combined with business.

Mental Health and Abilities

Contrary to popular belief (and barring disease), intelligence does not decline with age. While reaction speed does slow, some abilities such as judgment, accuracy and general knowledge may actually increase as learning continues. *Important:* Ongoing stimulation.

In terms of human development, one of the essential tasks of old age is to find ways to understand and use the lessons of one's lifetime. This entails learning to apportion one's strengths and resources, and to adapt to changes and losses as they occur.

Key: People must continue to adapt to stay healthy, both mentally and physically. Failure to adapt to changing circumstances can result in physical or mental illness at any age.

A comprehensive Seattle study found wide variation in intellectual changes among individuals as they aged. A large number showed little decline, even in their 80s. *What they had in common:* These people had no cardiovascular disease, were not poor, were actively involved in life…and their attitudes and behavior were already flexible in mid-life, and remained so.

Expect some emotional changes with aging. *Most common:* Family authority roles begin to reverse, usually in the mid-50s. Women tend to grow more active and assertive, while men tend to become more engendering or nurturant. This pattern occurs in many cultures and should be supported, as each sex explores potentials that may have been neglected in earlier life.

Recommended: Encourage men to share and network, women to be more self-determining and active in the world beyond their families.

Helpful to men: Beginning to recognize and develop your nurturant side now, whatever your age, can help to prevent or alleviate the common syndrome of stress, coronary disease and shortened life expectancy associated with overidentification with work and subsequent "retirement shock."

Other Changes to Expect— And Support

•Desire to leave a legacy. This can take many forms: Artwork, fortune, grandchildren, possessions, family recipes, memories in the minds of others. Many older people find the role of "elder" (counselor, mentor, teacher) to be particularly enriching.

•Altered sense of time. Older people tend to lose both "time panic" and boredom, in favor of a sense of time based on the appreciation of the truly important things in life…human relationships, nature, etc. *Result:* An ability to live in the moment that can make old age a richly enjoyable time, filled with emotional and sensory awareness. Older people also experience a personal sense of the cycle of life and one's place in the cycle…for many, a deepening of spiritual beliefs.

•Creativity and curiosity. Most older people stay productive and active their entire lives, barring ill health or social problems, such as poverty. *Less well known:* Many older people become creative for the first time in their lives. *Keys:* An attitude of curiosity and the ability to be surprised throughout one's lifetime.

•Feelings of serenity, wisdom, fulfillment. As older people come to accept the inevitability of death, feelings of satisfaction with one's life, of having done one's best, of having survived life's challenges, are more common than generally believed—though not as common as possible. The process of reminiscence that characterizes old age is essential to the emotional well-being of older people, as they work to resolve past conflicts and find significance in their life history.

Recommended: Pay attention to examining personal conflicts and reviewing one's life as a lifetime habit. Listen and support the process in the elderly. It can be hurtful, even devastating, for an older person to be told his/her life story is boring or unimportant.

Social Health

People who have healthy social networks have less disease and live longer than those who do not. A study of men and women over age 65 conducted at Duke University Medical Center found the risk of mortality to be four times greater in people who had little social support, even when other factors, such as gender, health, smoking, economic status, depression, etc., were considered.

A Swedish study found that social isolation is one of the best predictors of mortality from all causes. Other studies have found that individuals who are "self-starters," able to initiate new social contacts and activities, have the least disease and the longest survival rates.

Researchers are just starting to appreciate the importance of friendship at all phases of life. In addition to immediate family, friends are seen as "family" by many older persons, and they lend important support in times of need.

Studies are beginning to show that one reason women may outlive men is their greater skill in seeking and maintaining friendships. Mortality following the loss of a spouse is also lower in women, due, in part, to their better social networks.

Recommended: Use the telephone, write letters and cards, attend reunions. Nurture friendships with people of all ages throughout your lifetime. While many consider retirement communities to be artificially segregated environments, studies show older people who live among other older people make more friends than those who live among the young.

Caution: American cultural beliefs about independence and "doing for oneself" can foster a sense of isolation in people who resist help when it is needed. By contrast, people in group-oriented societies (Israeli kibbutzim, for example) can accept the support of others with no loss of self-esteem or feelings of dependence.

Recommended: Make use of support groups in the times of grief, stress or loss that are an inevitable part of life: Illness, widowhood, family crisis. *Also very useful:* Humor, a healing mechanism and coping skill that is underused in the elderly.

A Sense of Purpose

One's goal or purpose in later life (or any other time) need not be lofty. A sense of purpose can be derived from volunteer work, one's role as a grandparent or an attachment to the New York Yankees. Retirees who organize their daily lives to accommodate their goals live longer than those who do not.

Example: A University of Michigan study found that men who did volunteer work at least once a week were two-and-a-half times less likely to die than those who did none.

Caution: The highest suicide rate in America is among white men in their 80s. *Reason:* This group suffers the greatest loss of power, influence and status, and can therefore experience the greatest sense of helplessness and impotence.

Essential: Maintaining the deep sense of self-esteem that is derived from inner purpose.

Recommended: Begin now to make good use of your time...tutor, fund-raise, work for a cause you admire. *Key:* Choose a regularized activity that is outside yourself.

Source: Robert N. Butler, MD, chairman of the department of geriatrics at Mount Sinai School of Medicine, Mount Sinai Hospital, in New York City. Dr. Butler is co-author of *Aging and Mental Health*. Macmillan.

How to Have a Healthier Heart

Because cardiovascular disease is so familiar to all of us, we tend to think we know all about it. In fact, many ideas about heart disease commonly held by laypeople and physicians alike are nothing more than myths. *Included:*

•*Myth:* An aspirin a day prevents heart attacks. *Reality:* A daily aspirin tablet does seem to help people who have had one heart attack from having another—but there's very little benefit for those without pre-existing heart disease.

Recent study: For every 1,000 otherwise healthy people who took a daily aspirin tablet, heart attacks were prevented in only eight people. In contrast, 991 people experienced neither harm nor benefit...and one person suffered bleeding into the brain from the aspirin.

Aspirin has also been linked to stomach ulcers. And there is no evidence that taking a daily aspirin boosts life expectancy—people simply die from something other than a heart attack.

Self-defense: Do not take aspirin if your heart is healthy. If you have had a heart attack, take no more than one aspirin tablet a day—preferably children's aspirin.

•*Myth:* We should all try to lower our cholesterol levels. *Reality:* Special diets and cholesterol-lowering medications make sense only for certain people—hypertensives, smokers, diabetics, people with cholesterol levels 280 or above...and those already diagnosed with heart disease.

Note: Elevated cholesterol readings should be of little concern in healthy people aged 65 or older. Studies have shown that these elderly people are no longer at increased risk for heart attacks—if cholesterol hasn't led to heart disease by this age, it is probably no longer a threat.

•*Myth:* A prudent lifestyle virtually eliminates the risk of heart attacks. *Reality:* Adopting a healthy diet, losing weight and giving up smoking help prevent heart attacks, but nothing can guarantee a healthy heart.

Despite all kinds of precautions, some people wind up suffering a heart attack...just as others eat all the wrong foods and never exercise and remain healthy.

Bottom line: There is no way to eliminate your risk of heart disease entirely, even with the most aggressive preventive measures.

This does not mean a healthy lifestyle is of no value. I am a strong advocate of exercise and sensible diets, particularly from the standpoint of improved self-image.

•*Myth:* All hypertensives should avoid salt. *Reality:* Only about half of all cases of hypertension respond strongly to salt reduction. About 30% respond weakly. In about 20% of all cases, salt intake plays no role at all.

•*Myth:* A normal electrocardiogram (EKG) means a healthy heart. *Reality:* The EKG is an imperfect tool.

Although it's highly effective at pinpointing electrical disturbances in the heart and whether the patient is having or has ever had a heart attack, it reveals little about the health of the coronary arteries (the ones that sometimes clog and cause heart attacks).

Even hearts with severe blockages often appear normal on an EKG. I've had patients who had severe heart attacks within a week after having a normal EKG.

Alternative: The stress test. In this procedure, EKG readings are made during rigorous exercise on a treadmill. Stress tests are more likely to uncover potentially serious heart problems than are standard EKGs. However, even stress tests are not fail-safe.

•*Myth:* Heart murmurs are always dangerous. *Reality:* Although heart murmurs can be symptomatic of potentially deadly heart valve defects, they're often harmless.

In fact, a murmur means only that a physician using a stethoscope can hear blood rushing through the heart. This could mean a defective valve, but it's more likely the result of some other factor—a thin chest wall, pregnancy or even a highly conditioned heart.

If you are diagnosed with a heart murmur, make sure your doctor explains its nature—and whether or not you need to curtail physical activity.

•*Myth:* A normal blood-pressure reading means a healthy heart. *Reality:* There is no such thing as normal blood pressure. The lower your blood pressure, the lower your risk of stroke and heart disease. So even a very low blood pressure reading is generally a good thing.

But blood pressure readings are notoriously inaccurate. They can be thrown off by many things, including illness, anxiety, medications …even posture.

Doctors should always take several readings before confirming a case of hypertension. In some cases, the physician may ask the patient to wear a 24-hour blood-pressure monitor for a day.

•*Myth:* Bypass surgery restores the heart to good health. *Reality:* All it does is restore blood flow to parts of the heart that had been blood-deprived.

Bypass surgery may lower the risk of subsequent heart attacks and increase life expectancy. It cannot undo the effects of a previous heart attack. Damaged heart muscle remains damaged.

And unfortunately, the effects of bypass surgery do not last forever. Grafted blood vessels tend to clog back up within five to 10 years after surgery. Second and even third bypass operations are sometimes necessary.

If your physician recommends bypass surgery, find out how many blood vessels are diseased. If there are three or more, odds are you can benefit from bypass. For blockages in one or two coronary arteries, however, nonsurgical intervention is usually just as beneficial—and safer and less expensive.

Source: Bruce Charash, MD, assistant professor of medicine, Cornell University Medical College. A frequent lecturer on heart disease, Dr. Charash is the author of *Heart Myths*. Viking Penguin.

Tobacco Dangers

By now, most Americans are well aware that smoking causes lung cancer. But tobacco is a far bigger villain than most of us could ever imagine. Cigarettes, pipes, cigars, snuff and chewing tobacco kill more than 434,000 Americans each year—accounting for almost one out of five premature deaths in this country.

Lung cancer is just the first in a long and harrowing litany of tobacco-related problems.

Other Tobacco Dangers

•Addictiveness. While some people have likened the addictive potential of nicotine to that of heroin, the good news is that tens of millions of people have been trying to quit smoking.

•Back pain. Smoking is probably a major risk factor in recovery from back pain (the leading cause of worker disability in the US) because poor oxygen levels of those who smoke prevent lumbar disks from being adequately oxygenated.

•Bladder cancer. Smoking causes 40% of all cases of bladder cancer, accounting for more than 4,000 new cases annually.

•Breast cancer. Women who smoked heavily, more than one pack per day, and who started smoking at an early age are 75% more likely to develop breast cancer than nonsmoking women.

•Cervical cancer. Up to one third of all cases of cervical cancer—12,000 new cases a year—are directly attributable to smoking. Women who smoke are four times more likely to develop the disease than are nonsmoking women.

•Childhood respiratory ailments. Youngsters exposed to parents' tobacco smoke have six times as many respiratory infections as kids of nonsmoking parents. Smokers' children also face an increased risk of cough, chronic bronchitis and pneumonia.

•Diabetes. Smoking decreases the body's absorption of insulin. *Also:* Smoking exacerbates the damage of small blood vessels in the eyes, ears and feet of diabetics.

•Drug interactions. Smokers need higher than normal dosages of certain drugs, including theophylline (asthma medication), heparin (used to prevent blood clotting), propranolol (used for angina and high blood pressure) and medications for depression and anxiety.

•Ear infections. Children of smokers face an increased risk of otitis media (middle ear infection).

•Emphysema. Smoking accounts for up to 85% of all deaths attributable to emphysema.

•Esophageal cancer. Smoking accounts for 80% of all cases of esophageal cancer, which kills 15,000 Americans yearly.

•Financial woes. A pack of cigarettes (which costs the manufacturer less than 20¢!! to make) sells for about $3.70 a pack—nearly $1,350.50 a year for a pack-a-day user.

•Fires. Smoking is the leading cause of fires in homes, hotels and hospitals.

•Gastrointestinal cancer. Preliminary research indicates that smoking at least doubles the risk of cancer of the stomach and duodenum—the portion of the small intestine just downstream from the stomach.

•Heart disease. Smokers are up to four times more likely to develop cardiovascular disease than nonsmokers. *Mechanism:* Carbon monoxide and other poisonous gases in tobacco smoke replace oxygen in the blood cells, promote coronary spasm and cause accumulation of clot-producing platelets.

•Infertility. Couples in which at least one member smokes are more than three times as likely to have trouble conceiving than nonsmoking couples.

Explanation: Tobacco smoke interferes with the implantation of a fertilized egg within the uterus. It reduces the number and quality of sperm cells in a man's ejaculate and raises the number of abnormal sperm cells...and in-creases a man's risk of penile cancer. Women who smoke are more likely to miscarry or deliver prematurely than nonsmoking women. Some scientists now theorize that toxins in the bloodstream of pregnant smokers pass through the placenta to the fetus, sowing the seeds for future cancers.

•Kidney cancer. Smoking causes 40% of all cases of kidney cancer.

•Laryngeal cancer. Smokers who smoke more than 25 cigarettes a day are 25 to 30 times more likely to develop cancer of the larynx than nonsmokers.

•Leukemia. In addition to tobacco smoke condensate, better known as tar, tobacco smoke contains several powerful carcinogens, including the organic chemical benzene and a radioactive form of the element polonium, both of which can cause leukemia.

•Low birth weight. Women who smoke as few as five cigarettes daily during pregnancy face a significantly greater risk of giving birth to an unnaturally small, lightweight infant.

•Mouth cancer. Tobacco causes the vast majority of all cancers of the mouth, lips, cheek, tongue, salivary glands and even tonsils. Men who smoke, dip snuff or chew tobacco face a 27-fold risk of these cancers. Women smokers —because women have tended to use less tobacco—face a six-fold risk.

•Nutrition. People who smoke tend to have poorer nutrition than do nonsmokers. Smokers also have lower levels of HDL (good cholesterol).

•Occupational lung cancer. Although a nonsmoker's risk of lung cancer increases six times due to prolonged occupational exposure to asbestos, that risk jumps to 92 times in an asbestos worker who smokes.

•Osteoporosis. Women who smoke experience menopause on an average of five to 10 years earlier than nonsmokers, causing a decline in estrogen production—and thinning bones—at an earlier age.

•Pharyngeal (throat) cancer. Cancer of the pharynx kills thousands of Americans each year—the majority of these deaths the direct result of smoking.

•Premature aging. Constant exposure to tobacco smoke prematurely wrinkles facial skin and yellows the teeth and fingernails.

•Recovery from injury or surgery. Wound and bone injuries of smokers take a longer period of time to heal. Smokers also have a greater risk of complications from surgery, including pneumonia (due to weaker lungs), and remain in the hospital for longer periods.

•Stroke. Smoking increases the risk of stroke two-fold both among men and women.

Special danger: For women who smoke and use oral contraceptives, the risk of stroke is increased 10-fold.

•Tooth loss. Use of snuff or chewing tobacco causes gum recession and tooth abrasion, two frequent contributors to tooth loss.

Source: Alan Blum, MD, family physician, Department of Family Medicine, Baylor College of Medicine, Houston. Dr. Blum is the founder and president of Doctors Ought to Care (DOC), c/o Department of Family Medicine, Baylor College of Medicine, 5510 Greenbriar, Houston 77005, an antismoking group long-recognized for its service to public health.

When Chest Pain Means Heart Attack and When It Doesn't

Chest pain is psychosomatic almost half the time, according to a recent study. *Key:* If the pain is sharp and stabbing, or it's on the left side of the chest, it's likely caused by psychological stress. But a heavy, gripping sensation in the central chest is a typical heart attack symptom, especially if it lasts five to six minutes. Consult your doctor in either case.

Source: Study by Dr. Christopher Bass, King's College Hospital, London.

How to Handle the Catastrophic Health-Care Problem Now

Amazing as it seems, two thirds of all people since the beginning of time who have ever lived beyond age 65 are alive today.

What's more, the average person who lives to be 65 today will live to be 87. *Staggering implication:* That person will have to finance 22 years of retirement in sickness or in health. It's estimated that 30 million Americans—15 million of them now working—have no medical insurance at all. And, many others are seriously underprotected. *New realities in health care:*

•Hospital and medical costs are going up at an alarming rate because of expensive new medical technology, inflation and high medical malpractice insurance rates that doctors must pay.

•Strained by the budget deficit, the government has been reducing its role in health care. It has toughened Medicare payment standards, raised premiums for people over 65 and tightened eligibility requirements for Medicaid coverage of the poor. It's also trying to shift some of the burden for health-care costs to the private sector by, for example, requiring employer health plans to pay benefits to any employees before Medicare kicks in.

•Companies, trying desperately to cut costs and remain globally competitive, are trying to shift health costs to their employees by means of higher deductibles, co-payments and shared premiums. *Most vulnerable:* Retirement health benefits for current employees. Some companies simply won't offer them. Others will make employees pay a big share of the cost.

•Insurers, faced with the spectre of such catastrophic illnesses as AIDS, which now costs about $250,000 per patient, will surely toughen underwriting standards as much as allowed by law. Where they're permitted to give applicants blood tests, they'll not only screen out those carrying the AIDS virus but may also uncover other medical conditions that will cause them to refuse coverage or charge extra premiums.

What to Do Now

Put health insurance at the top of your priority list. If you don't have it through an employer, talk to your insurance agent and select a comprehensive health-care policy from a strong (rated A+ excellent by A.M. Best) company with a good reputation for paying claims. Having a respected agent behind you can often help in getting insurance and claims service.

Costs: For an individual in his or her late 30s, good medical comprehensive coverage can be had for $1,500–$2,000. For a family of four, with the parents in their 40s, it will cost closer to $6,000.

Coverage Everyone Needs

•Basic hospital insurance. The Blue Cross program is the best-known hospital insurer nationally, but it really consists of local entities that vary in service from place to place. *What you'll want covered:* A semi-private hospital room with meals, general nursing services, in-hospital lab and x-ray fees, operating room costs, in-hospital medications and various other in-hospital expenses.

Trap: The average hospital stay right now is only about nine days. Thus, it's a mistake to pay for insurance only on the basis of how many hospital days it will reimburse you for. Also, find out what the insurance company's definition of "in-hospital" is because many procedures are now performed on an outpatient basis and you'll need coverage for these, too.

•Surgical medical coverage. This covers visits to doctors, including any necessary operations. Again, Blue Shield is the best-known nationally, but many other companies offer similar policies. Blue Cross and Blue Shield can be somewhat cheaper because they are nonprofit companies, but some of their tax advantage was removed by tax reform, so they don't have as great a cost advantage as they used to.

•Major medical. This is critical because it picks up after the relatively low limits on the first two types of insurance and acts as a kind of umbrella coverage to protect you if you are struck by a major illness or injury, such as cancer or a heart attack. Look for a policy that pays up to $1 million or more because any major problem these days can run into thousands of dollars.

Use Big Deductibles

The best way to get the most protection for the least premium dollar is to take big deductibles. Ask yourself how much of the initial cost of an illness or hospitalization you can afford to bear without creating a severe long-term financial hardship. Most people could probably afford a deductible of $750 on a major medical policy, for example. After the deductible, look for coverage that pays at least 80% of expenses up to a level of, say, $2,000–$5,000 and then 100% thereafter.

Important: Find out whether the deductible is a "per-cause" or "calendar-year" or "benefit-year" type. An all-cause calendar-year or benefit-year deductible is preferable because you would then be reimbursed at any point when your total covered medical expenses for the year reached the deductible. In the following year, you would be responsible for another deductible.

Medigap Insurance

Those over 65 on Medicare need supplemental private insurance called Medigap. This generally covers the basic Medicare in-hospital deductible plus some portion of the many extras that Medicare doesn't cover or covers to only a limited extent, e.g., doctor's bills that are above Medicare's limits. One of the best Medigap policies is offered by the American Association of Retired Persons (AARP). The company has already announced that its Medicare Supplement Plans will probably adjust benefits (and premiums) to make up for cutbacks in Medicare. No doubt it will continue to fill those gaps. And if not, other companies will.

Nursing-Home Care

The most frightening aspect of growing older is the possibility of having to spend many months or years in a nursing home or an extended-care facility. Current statistics show that 40% of people over 65 will need care in a nursing home at some time in the future. The average cost for long-term nursing-home care could range from $45,000 to $100,000 a year depending on location. Costs for long-term care at home could be half that amount, depending on the area and level of care received.

Depressing: A recent study estimated that 80% of single people and 55% of married people over 65 in nursing homes will have impoverished themselves. After two years, the number rises to nearly 90% for both groups. But Medicare basically doesn't cover long-term nursing-home or at-home care. Even Medicaid, the joint federal and state program to provide a safety net for those with low incomes or high medical bills, will pick up the tab only after you've exhausted nearly all of your own assets (except your home) and those of your spouse.

Result: Some 100 companies are now marketing nursing-home or long-term care insurance. It's one of the hottest insurance products today, although it's not cheap.

What to look for: Get a policy that is guaranteed renewable for life, with a grace period of seven to 31 days in case premiums are paid late. Some offer an inflation protection option. Ask on what basis premiums will be increased.

Try to find a policy that does not require prior hospitalization and that does provide coverage for skilled, intermediate or custodial care without requiring licensed medical professionals. That's key for getting help caring for Alzheimer's patients, for example. *Trap:* Make sure that Alzheimer's is covered. It's called an organically based mental condition, and if that's not mentioned, it may not be covered.

Leading companies offering this insurance: CNA, GE Capital and Travelers.

When to buy: Generally, not before your 50s, but if you buy then you may be able to get a more favorable premium later on. Certainly consider it when you're 60. Then you can rest assured that if serious or prolonged illness strikes, it won't bankrupt your family.

Source: Sam E. Beller, CLU, ChFC, is president of Diversified Programs, Inc., 450 Seventh Ave., New York 10123. He is an insurance agent and a financial planner and is the author of *The Great Insurance Secret.* William Morrow.

Fat Removal Technique

Liposuction—surgery performed to remove excess fat from various parts of the body—is now the most popular cosmetic operation in the United States. The doctor inserts a thin tube called a *cannula* through a small incision in the skin and moves it back and forth to break up a fatty deposit. The dislodged fat is then evacuated through this tubing by strong suction.

In cases where a person has good skin elasticity—up into their early 40s for most people —a double chin can be fixed without undergoing a face lift. Liposuction can remove fat from a full neck, giving the patient a clean jawline and only a tiny scar.

Source: Dr. Henry Zackin, a plastic and reconstructive surgeon in private practice in New York City.

How to Get the Government Aid That You are Entitled to for Health Care and Medical Bills

Given the skyrocketing costs of medical care and health insurance, it is particularly important to make sure you receive the benefits you're entitled to...and to minimize the expenses for which you are liable.

The primary federal health-care programs are Medicare...and Medicaid—for the needy.

Other government programs, for which fewer people are eligible, include Veterans Administration (VA) benefits and Supplemental Security Income (SSI).

Medicare is a tax-funded insurance program you have paid premiums for—through Social Security—and that you are entitled to.

Even with an employer-provided health-insurance plan—and we recommend you keep any plan you have—you should enroll in Medicare Part A (hospital insurance), when you turn 65...and purchase Part B (doctor insurance) within three months of your 65th birthday. Otherwise, you will have to pay an additional 10% premium for every year you wait. Enrolling keeps that cost to your employer down and maximizes the benefits of your existing plan.

Medicare was never intended to cover all of its beneficiaries' health costs. Everyone's share is rising. Today, the elderly spend up to 20% of their income on health care, even with Medicare.

Money-saving solutions: Make sure you have supplemental private insurance ("Medigap" coverage)...and try to keep all medical costs as low as possible.

How to Get the Most from Medicare

Maximize your coverage by tuning into Medicare's best-kept secrets...

•Doctors' fees are very negotiable. A doctor who accepts Medicare assignments agrees to accept the fee that it pays for the procedure or treatments provided and handles the paperwork. You remain responsible for your deductible and 20% co-payment.

Seventy-five percent of physicians and other limited licensed practitioners accept assignments for all of their Medicare patients. Ninety percent of all Medicare-allowed charges are now billed by participating practitioners. This shows how consumers have used their power to persuade providers to accept assignment.

If your physician does not accept assignment, you can try to persuade him. *Helpful approach:* "I believe that Medicare pays a fair rate, and I hope you will respect my request, as I cannot afford more than the 20% co-payment. However, if you do not accept assignments, perhaps you could refer me to another practitioner who does." Doctors do not like to lose clients. Most people who take the trouble to negotiate assignments are successful.

•You never have to pay more than the balance billing limit for any service, even if your doctor does not take assignments.

Medicare has set a maximum fee of 115% above the Medicare-approved amount for all services that doctors who do not take assignments may charge Medicare patients. (Some states have an even lower limit.) To find out a specific balance billing limit, call the Medicare carrier in your area. If your doctor bills you for more than the balance billing limit, neither you nor your insurance company has to pay the difference.

Example: Your doctor charges $3,000 for a procedure. Medicare pays $2,000 for the same procedure, and has set the balance billing limit at $2,300. Medicare will pay 80% of the $2,000 "reasonable cost," or $1,600. If your doctor accepts assignments, you would only have to pay the 20% co-payment, or $400. If the doctor does not take assignments, you must pay the difference between $1,600 and the $2,300 balance billing limit, or $700, and the doctor must absorb the other $700. (The difference between the doctor's charge of $3,000 and the balance billing limit of $2,300.) But if you didn't check the balance billing limit, you may be billed for the full $3,000, less Medicare's $1,600, and unknowingly pay the $1,400 difference.

•The fact that Medicare refuses payment does not necessarily mean that you must pay.

You are not responsible for any medical bill that you could not reasonably have been expected to know wasn't covered. You must be informed in writing from an official source, such as a Medicare notice or pamphlet, that a service isn't covered. If your doctor tells you something is covered by Medicare and it isn't, then the doctor—neither you nor your insurer—is responsible.

•You cannot be discharged from the hospital before you are medically able to go. You cannot be discharged because your Medicare payments or "DRG" (Diagnosis-Related Group system) days have been used up. When you are admitted to the hospital, you will be issued a form outlining your rights as a Medicare patient. If you think you are being discharged too soon, request a review by your state's PRO (Peer Review Organization), a group of doctors who review Medicare cases. The PRO will decide if your Medicare coverage can be extended, based on medical necessity.

Shopping for "Medigap" Insurance

Employer-provided retiree health insurance is usually as good as the available high-option Medigap policies, and often better. But several million Medicare beneficiaries continue to purchase duplicate policies to supplement their Medicare coverage. Changes in the law prohibit an insurance company from *knowingly* selling a second or third Medigap policy to a Medicare beneficiary. *Unfortunately,* these companies are not prohibited from selling *disease-specific* insurance (such as cancer, heart, accident) to Medicare beneficiaries. If you have an employer-sponsored plan you may not need more coverage. If not, consider supplemental insurance. *What to look for...*

The federal government certifies insurance policies as meeting the standards established for Medicare Supplemental Insurance or "Medigap" policies. As a result of reforms in the Medigap insurance market, one basic policy and a number of other optional plans have been approved for sale. It is illegal for an insurance company to sell you a policy as a Medigap plan if it does not conform to these standards.

Key: Since the coverage offered by each plan is the same regardless of the insurance company selling it, the only difference is the premium. Comparison shop on premium, once you have determined which plan best meets your needs. Also, be aware that all of the different types of Medigap policies may not be available in your state. Check with your state insurance department to learn which policies are approved in your state and which companies are authorized to sell policies.

If you have had a Medigap policy for at least six months and you switch policies, the replacement policy may not impose a waiting period for any pre-existing conditions. *The only exception:* Your new policy offers a benefit that was not in the old policy. However, some states prohibit any exclusions.

Rule of thumb: Don't change an existing policy unless you know that your new policy will cover your existing conditions.

Saving on Out-of-Pocket Expenses

You can minimize your co-payments and keep premiums down by trying to keep your medical expenses as low as possible.

•Take advantage of low-cost or free health services offered by counties, organizations or health fairs.

Examples: Inoculations, screenings.

•Make sure you are aware of your health plan's limits and exclusions.

Example: Number of chiropractic visits.

•Shop around for prescription prices and buy generic drugs when possible.

•Guard against unnecessary or excessive testing. Many physicians have adopted new, costly tests while continuing to administer the old ones—often less expensive and as effective.

•Avoid hospitalization and surgery unless absolutely necessary. Avoid for-profit hospitals—they're up to 23% more costly. Avoid weekend admission.

•Bring your own food, vitamins and drugs.

•Specify in writing that surgery or invasive procedures must be done by the person you are paying, i.e., your fully-trained physician, not a resident or intern.

•Keep track of all bills and services while hospitalized.

Common errors to check for: Additional services not covered by the DRG for your condition, physician visits that actually occurred, as opposed to those routinely billed. Report any irregularities to the Medicare Inspector General at 800-447-8477.

Source: Charles B. Inlander, president of the People's Medical Society, a nonprofit consumers' health organization, 462 Walnut St., Allentown, PA 18102. His book, coauthored with Karla Morales, is *Getting the Most for Your Medical Dollar*. Pantheon.

Helping Yourself to Sleep Better

As the stress of doing business under unsettled conditions continues month after month, the sleeping patterns of executives with top responsibilities become more and more unraveled. Late meetings, travel and racing thoughts that produce late-night or morning insomnia result in irritability, poor work performance and lethargy at times when key decisions must be made.

Improving Sleep Quality

Researchers cannot easily determine how much sleep is optimum for a specific person. But they have determined that, on average, people need seven or eight hours of sleep a day.

The evidence is clear, however, that psychological and physical health improves as the quality of sleep is enhanced. *To sleep better, you should:*

•Determine the right amount of sleep. *How:* Keep a diary of sleeping patterns for at least 10–14 days. If you feel productive and alert, the average sleep time during that period is probably the amount you need.

•Establish a regular bedtime and wake-up schedule, then stick to it even on weekends and holidays.

•Avoid trying to make up for loss of sleep one night by sleeping more the next. Sleep deprivation of two to four hours does not severely affect performance. Having the normal amount of sleep the next night compensates for the loss without changing the regular sleep pattern. And that has long-term benefits.

•Relax before bedtime. *Good ways to unwind:* Take a bath, read, have a snack (milk is ideal for many people), engage in sex. Avoid late-night exercise, work, arguments and activities that cause tension.

Fighting Insomnia

Knowing the reason for insomnia is the only way to start overcoming it. If the cause is not quickly obvious, see a doctor. Many emotional and physical disorders express themselves as sleep disturbances.

Avoid sleeping pills. On a long-term basis, they are useless and sometimes dangerous. And when taken infrequently, they may produce a drug hangover the next day.

Catnaps

Avoid naps in the middle of the day to compensate for lack of sleep the previous night. Take them only if you do so regularly and feel refreshed instead of groggy after a nap. *Test:* If you dream during a catnap, it is likely to delay sleep that evening or cause insomnia.

Tampering with Nature

Deliberate attempts to reduce the total amount of sleep you need have a dangerous appeal to hard-pressed executives who think they never have enough time to work. *Fact:* Carefully researched evidence from monitoring subjects in sleep laboratories indicates that these schemes are not only ineffective but unhealthful. *Why:* The daily biological cycle cannot be changed by gradually cutting back sleep over a period of months. Older persons apparently need slightly less sleep, but even here the exact difference is not yet known.

Hard-to-take but essential advice: Do not cut down on sleep in order to meet the clamoring and sometimes conflicting demands of a job, family and friends. You may pay a penalty of spending less time with family and friends or losing the edge at work that compulsive workaholism may provide. But the payoff is better health performance.

Source: Dr. Charles P. Pollak, codirector, Sleep-Wake Disorders Center, Montefiore Hospital, New York.

Harmful Denture Adhesives

Denture adhesives can actually be more harmful than helpful to users. Karaya gum, a common ingredient, is highly acidic and eats away the enamel of natural teeth. Constant use may dissolve bone tissue and promote fungus infections in the mouth. *The good news:* Properly fitting dentures don't require adhesives in the first place.

Source: Dr. George Murrell, University of Southern California, Los Angeles 90007.

What Nourishes and What Poisons Friendship

Key Nourishing Qualities

•Authenticity. Inauthentic behavior is contrived and false. Authentic behavior is spontaneous and unpremeditated. Being freely and deeply oneself is important to friendship.

•Acceptance. A sound friendship permits the expression of anger, childishness and silliness. It allows us to express the various facets of our personality without fear of harsh judgment. A feeling of being valued promotes our fullest functioning with other people.

•Direct expression. Coaxing, cajoling, dropping "cute" hints, manipulating and beating around the bush are all barriers to clear communications. When people know what they want from each other, they establish clear communication and contact. They're in a position to attempt an agreement regarding their desires. They may also realize they're too different to get along and that they may be less frustrated if their relationship is more casual.

•Empathy. This involves an effort to understand another's beliefs, practices and feelings (not necessarily agreeing with them). Empathy means listening, trying to understand and communicating this understanding to the speaker.

What Poisons Friendships

•Blame. Blame shifts responsibility and also can be a way of avoiding self-examination. The antithesis of blame and defensiveness is to assume responsibility for one's own feelings. If a person is honest enough to admit his mistakes and finds he's forgiven, he can then be tolerant of his friends' foibles.

•Excess dependency. Some people have lost touch with their values and their strength and need other people to lean on. This kind of person feels unable to be alone. In the dependent friendship, growth and development are stifled rather than enhanced.

Source: Dr. Joel D. Block, clinical psychologist and author of *Friendship: How to Give It, How to Get It.* Macmillan.

How to Change Your Biological Age

Gray hair, wrinkled skin, growing flabbiness and reduced resistance to injury and disease...

To most Americans, these are harbingers of old age, unwelcome but inevitable milestones along a path that leads inexorably to the grave.

In fact, recent research suggests that the body's gradual decline stems not from the passing of years but from the combined effects of inactivity and poor nutrition. So no matter what your present health status or your chronological age, regular exercise and improved eating habits will lower your biological age.

Benefits: Reduced body fat...increased muscle mass...strength increases of 200% to 300% ...increases in aerobic capacity of 20% or more ...and reduced risk of heart disease, diabetes, osteoporosis and other age-related ailments.

To lose fat and gain muscle: Be sure to combine a low-fat diet with regular exercise.

•Aerobic capacity. To gauge fitness, doctors often measure the body's ability to process oxygen during exercise. The greater this aerobic capacity, the faster oxygen is pumped throughout the body—and the fitter the individual. Like other biomarkers, aerobic capacity often declines with age. Typically, by age 65 it is 30% to 40% below its level in young adulthood.

•Blood-sugar tolerance. For most Americans, aging brings about a gradual decline in the body's ability to metabolize blood sugar (glucose). So common is this problem that by age 70, 20% of men and 30% of women are at an increased risk of diabetes, a potential killer.

At special risk for problems: The overweight, the sedentary and those who eat a fatty diet.

Good news: A low-fat, high-fiber diet, combined with regular exercise, will cut your diabetes risk. Be sure to include both strength-building and aerobic exercise in your routine.

•Cholesterol ratio. As most of us know, high cholesterol boosts your risk of heart disease. But total cholesterol isn't the only thing that counts.

Very important: The ratio of total cholesterol to HDL (good cholesterol). For older people, the ideal ratio is 4.5 or lower. A person whose total cholesterol is 200 and whose HDL is 50, for example, has a ratio of 200/50, or 4.0.

To lower your ratio: Stop smoking, lose weight, reduce your intake of fatty, cholesterol-rich foods and exercise regularly.

•Blood pressure. In many parts of the world, advancing age brings little if any change in blood pressure. In the US, however, where older people tend to be both overweight and sedentary, blood pressure does rise with age.

To keep pressure in check: Stay slim, don't smoke, get regular exercise and limit your consumption of fat, salt and alcohol. If these steps fail to regulate pressure, pressure-lowering drugs may be necessary.

•Bone density. As we age, our skeletons slowly become weaker and more brittle. While some mineral loss is inevitable, the severe and potentially deadly condition known as osteoporosis is not.

Prevention: Although consuming at least 800 milligrams of calcium a day will retard the loss of bone, that alone rarely does the trick. *Also needed:* Weight-bearing exercise, such as walking, running or cycling. *Not helpful:* Swimming and other forms of exercise that do not subject the long bones to the stress of gravity.

•Body temperature regulation. Compared with young people, old people sweat less, get less thirsty and excrete more water in their urine. These seemingly minor changes, which are a part of aging—plus the loss of muscle tissue needed for efficient shivering—hinder the body's ability to regulate its internal temperature, which raises our risk of dehydration in summer and hypothermia in winter.

Source: William J. Evans, PhD, chief of the human physiology lab at the Human Nutrition Research Center on Aging, a Boston-based facility operated jointly by the US Department of Agriculture and Tufts University. Dr. Evans is the coauthor of *Biomarkers: The 10 Keys for Prolonging Vitality.* Fireside Books.

CHAPTER SEVEN

Medical Problems and Solutions

Leg Cramp Reliever

Nighttime leg-cramp relief: "Acupinch." *How it works:* With thumb and forefinger, pinch your upper lip—yes, lip—just below the nose for 20 to 30 seconds. This works about 80% of the time.

Source: Donald Cooper, former US Olympic team doctor, quoted in *Minute Health Tips: Medical Advice and Facts at a Glance* by Thomas G. Welch, MD. DCI/Chronimed Publishing.

Heart-Attack Self-Defense

Before using CPR, call 911—if an adult is having a heart attack. Doctors used to recommend that trained rescuers give one minute of cardiopulmonary resuscitation before calling the emergency number. *New finding:* Survival and recovery rates are better if 911 is called first. *Important exception:* For children under age eight, a trained rescuer should use proper techniques before calling 911. All untrained rescuers should call 911 immediately.

Source: Emergency Cardiac Care Committee and subcommittee, American Heart Association, guidelines for cardiopulmonary resuscitation and emergency cardiac care, reported in *Journal of American Medical Association,* 515 N. State St., Chicago 60610.

Smoking and Alzheimer's

In a health study conducted by Harvard University, it was observed that individuals who smoked more than one pack of cigarettes a day were four times as likely to develop Alzheimer's disease as those who smoked less. *Reason:* Unknown...

Source: Stuart L. Shalat, ScD, assistant professor of epidemiology and medicine, Yale University School of Medicine.

Misdiagnosed Alzheimer's Disease

•Pernicious anemia, a vitamin B_{12} deficiency that can cause memory loss, paranoia, dementia, and paralysis, is sometimes thought to be Alzheimer's. *Trap:* People over 65 can have it without even knowing. *Reason:* The usual test for the condition—a blood test—identifies the vitamin deficiency only after neurological damage has occurred. A new urine test, however, detects it before it can do any damage. *Cost:* $70. *Availability:* Only through the test's developer, Eric J. Norman, PhD, Norman Clinical Laboratory, 1044 Sunwood Ct., Cincinnati, OH 45231, 800-397-7408.

•Signs of senility caused by hypothyroidism (low hormone output by the thyroid gland) are treatable. *Problem:* The disorder is often confused with Alzheimer's disease. Symptoms include memory loss, depression, deafness, weight loss, weakness, constipation, and incontinence.

Source: *Healthwise.*

Tranquilizers and Hip Fractures

Elderly people who take tranquilizers that remain in the body for more than 24 hours are 70% more likely to fracture their hips in falls than those taking tranquilizers that remain in the body for less than 24 hours or those who don't take any at all. *Long-acting:* Diazepam, Flurazepam, chlordiazepoxide. *Short-acting:* Alprazolam, lorazepam, oxazepam.

Source: T. Franklin Williams, MD, director, National Institute on Aging, Bethesda, MD.

Stroke News

Stroke, which afflicts 750,000 people in the US each year...and kills 250,000, ranks as the third-leading cause of death, after heart disease and cancer.

Although the number of strokes declined through the 1960s and 1970s, data from the 1980s shows that this decline has leveled off.

The number of strokes declined because doctors developed new ways to treat high blood pressure—a common cause of stroke—and people became more aware of the dangers of smoking and the importance of exercising.

Now, however, as the population ages, the incidence of stroke is increasing. *Reason:* Although strokes can affect people of any age, most occur in people over age 60.

New goal: To find new ways to prevent strokes ...or at least to make them less severe if they do occur.

What Happens

A stroke is a sudden decrease in the blood supply to a portion of the brain. That portion of the brain which is affected dies.

Most strokes are caused by blocked arteries or high blood pressure. *What happens:* Blood flow to the brain is blocked by a narrow or closed artery…a small blood clot travels to the brain…a blood vessel in the brain ruptures…or an aneurysm—a bulge in an artery—ruptures.

Getting Help

People should seek emergency medical care and a complete neurological exam if they experience any of the following symptoms:

•Sudden paralysis or numbness on one side of the body.

•Difficulty speaking.

•Difficulty seeing.

•A severe headache—either the worst headache ever or a bad headache in someone who never gets headaches.

One of the biggest problems with stroke is that people who are having one often don't seek treatment right away. And delays can make the problem much, much worse.

Some people have so-called mini-strokes—they only suffer symptoms for a few minutes…and then they feel better. *Trap:* These people may be at increased risk for a major stroke.

Even people who experience very serious symptoms that don't go away take between three and six hours to go to the hospital after a stroke. Although part of the delay may be attributed to confusion or to difficulty communicating or moving, the person is usually just denying that something so terrible could really be happening.

Warning: A person who experiences any symptoms of a stroke should immediately call his/her doctor or go to the nearest emergency room.

Emergency Treatment

At the emergency room, a doctor will take the person's history and perform a physical examination to determine the urgency of the situation. Vital signs will be checked, including blood pressure.

A CAT scan of the brain can show signs of stroke and allow the doctor to investigate the small chance that the symptoms may be caused by another problem, like a tumor. The patient will be given oxygen and intravenous feeding in order to prevent dehydration.

Drug Therapy

Standard therapies:

•Aspirin. Many doctors are now recommending that some patients over age 50 with risk factors for stroke take one aspirin a day as a preventive measure. Aspirin thins the blood, making it less likely for a clot to form in the brain. *Note:* Aspirin is not recommended immediately after a stroke. *Reason:* It may result in bleeding into the brain around the area of the stroke.

Drawbacks: Although aspirin is cheap and reliable, it can cause a peptic ulcer or bleeding from the gastrointestinal tract. For this reason, patients should consult their doctors before starting aspirin therapy.

Doctors may prescribe specially coated aspirin to prevent ulcers from developing. Anyone taking aspirin every day who develops stomach pain, vomits blood or finds blood in his stools should be screened for ulcers.

•Heparin. This anti-coagulant can be used to prevent stroke and occasionally to treat an acute stroke.

Drawbacks: This type of therapy is much riskier than aspirin in terms of consequences from bleeding and may not be any better in preventing a stroke. Heparin is generally given only in hospitals because it requires intravenous (IV) administration.

Some patients who need to be on chronic anti-coagulant therapy are also prescribed an oral medication, warfarin (*trade name:* Coumadin).

This chronic medical therapy is reserved for patients with certain heart conditions—chronic irregularities of the heart rhythm or artificial mechanical heart valves—that predispose them to strokes.

•Nimodipine. Has been successfully used to treat strokes in which a blood vessel bursts—approximately 10% of all strokes. Nimodipine prevents spasm of the blood vessels in the brain region of the stroke—a significant problem after an aneurysm ruptures.

Drawbacks: Nimodipine may cause a significant drop in blood pressure, which may bring on a stroke, or make a stroke worse. There is not yet enough research data to recommend the use of nimodipine in the majority of stroke patients who do not have rupture of an aneurysm. In the future, this medication may be used on a broader range of stroke victims.

Experimental therapies:

•Ticlopidine. A new agent that works like aspirin but may or may not be any better than aspirin in preventing strokes.

Drawbacks: Adverse side effects that aspirin does not have—low white blood cell counts in some patients and elevated cholesterol levels. Considering its adverse effects, ticlopidine cannot yet be recommended as a replacement for aspirin.

•Rt-PA and streptokinase. Researchers are trying to determine if patients with strokes can be helped by these blood-thinning agents, now used during heart attacks to dissolve clots in the coronary artery. *Assumption:* If we can immediately dissolve the clot causing the stroke, we can reduce the damage. Rt-PA and streptokinase take only about a minute to work.

Drawback: 1% of heart attack patients given rt-PA or streptokinase will develop a stroke. Because it may cause worsening of the stroke from bleeding, this type of therapy cannot yet be recommended for stroke patients except under certain experimental protocols.

•Ancrod—an enzyme extracted from the Malaysian pit viper, which may enhance blood flow to areas of the brain that are affected by stroke. It is currently available only through experimental research protocols. Ancrod may herald the event of a number of other similar types of therapies in an area of research that's known as biorheological therapy. This involves methods to enhance cerebral blood flow by reducing blood viscosity. *Other similar measures now being investigated:*

•Expanding blood volume to increase cerebral blood flow using certain IV fluids.

•Pentoxifylline (*trade name:* Trental), which increases the ability of red blood cells that carry oxygen to reach distant parts of the brain despite narrowed blood vessels. Trental has been used for years to treat patients with circulation problems in the legs, but its efficacy in treating strokes has yet to be proven.

•Prostacyclin, a medication that is a prostaglandin. Prostaglandins—fatty acids found in virtually all body tissues—have numerous and often contradictory effects upon many bodily functions. *Example:* They can both increase and decrease blood flow to the brain through many mechanisms. This type of therapy is still in early experimental stages, but may one day be useful in affecting the basic underlying mechanisms causing strokes.

Prevention

Of course, the best way to minimize damage from strokes is to prevent them in the first place. *Best:*

•Eat a diet that is low in fat.

•Exercise regularly.

•Eliminate risk factors such as being overweight and smoking.

•See a doctor on a routine basis for blood-pressure checks. Seek regular treatment if you have medical risk factors, such as diabetes or heart disease.

•Don't take oral contraceptives if you smoke. If you live with a smoker, consult your doctor to determine whether or not contraceptives are safe for you.

•Avoid over-the-counter diet pills. Most contain ingredients that increase the risk of stroke.

Finally, people who have aneurysms can elect to have surgical treatment that can prevent stroke.

What happens: Blood flow to the aneurysm is prevented with the placement of a permanent metal clip at the base of the aneurysm that allows blood to flow normally through the rest of the artery.

Source: Gary P. Young, MD, FACEP, FACP, director, emergency department, Veterans Affairs Medical Center, US Veterans Hospital Road, Portland, OR 97207. Dr. Young recently edited a special report on strokes for the medical journal, *Emergency Medicine Reports.*

Unnecessary Cataract Surgery

Unless cataracts interfere with normal activities, surgery isn't recommended. *Trap:* Many doctors routinely remove cataracts before it's truly necessary. Because cataracts vary in size, density and location in the lens, they can exist for a lifetime without creating major vision problems. *Time for surgery:* When you can't read a newspaper because of cataracts.

Source: Dr. Stephen Bloomfield, associate professor of ophthalmology at Cornell University Medical School.

Pneumonia Self-Defense

Pneumonia/hospital connection: About two-thirds of all elderly pneumonia patients studied had been hospitalized within the past four years—for one illness or another. *Recommended:* Because many of these pneumonias are caused by pneumococcal infection, all people older than the age of 65 should have a pneumococcal vaccine following a hospital stay to protect against pneumonia. *Advantage:* The cost of a vaccination is approximately one-third the cost of hospital care for unvaccinated patients who are readmitted suffering from pneumonia.

Source: David S. Fedson, MD, professor of internal medicine, University of Virginia School of Medicine, Charlottesville.

Relieving Arthritis Pain

•Vegetable and fish oils can reduce arthritis pain. Polyunsaturated (vegetable) fats and eicosapentanoic acid (found in fish oil) relieve arthritis pain by producing a less inflammatory hormone than saturated (animal) fats.

Source: Albany Medical College, State University of New York, Albany, NY 12246.

•A fat-rich diet makes arthritis patients feel worse. When the patients in a recent study avoided red meat and other foods high in polyunsaturated fats, they reported less joint pain and morning stiffness.

Also helpful: Fish oil supplements.

Source: *The Lancet.*

Silent Heart Attacks

Many victims of heart disease are unaware of their problem because they suffer painless heart attacks. *Most vulnerable:* People who smoke or have high blood pressure or a high cholesterol level. *Protection:* People with one or more of these traits should undergo tests that detect susceptibility to painless attacks. If the potential is there, preventive drugs can be prescribed.

Source: Dr. Peter F. Cohn, chief of cardiology, State University of New York Health Sciences Center, quoted in *Venture.*

Exercise vs. Breast Cancer

Women who averaged four or more hours of exercise a week had a 58% lower risk of breast cancer than non-exercisers. Exercising one to three hours a week cut the risk by 20% to 30%.

Theory: Exercise alters levels of hormones that play major roles in the development of breast cancer.

Source: Leslie Bernstein, MD, professor of preventive medicine, University of Southern California, Los Angeles.

Diet vs. Colorectal Cancer

Reduce your risk of colorectal cancer by eating a diet high in fiber *and* calcium. Ninety people at risk for colorectal cancer were given varying doses of calcium and wheat bran fiber supplements. *Result:* The high-fiber group (13.5 g per day) produced 52% less bile acid than did the low-fiber group. Those who consumed the most calcium (15,000 mg) had a 35% reduction in bile acid production.

Theory: Fiber and calcium soak up these cancer-promoting acids. One ounce of Kellogg's All-Bran contains 10 g of fiber...and one cup of milk contains 300 mg of calcium.

Source: David Alberts, MD, director of Cancer Prevention and Control at the Arizona Cancer Center in Tucson.

Lowering Your Cholesterol

Cholesterol-lowering drug *colestipol* (Colestid) can be used more economically *and* more effectively when mixed with the natural fiber supplement *psyllium.* Patients who took half (2.5 g) their usual dosage of colestipol, plus 2.5 g of psyllium, had greater declines in the all-important cholesterol-to-HDL ratio than when they took colestipol alone. Fewer side effects were reported with the mixture, too. Consult your doctor first.

Source: J. David Spence, MD, director, Stroke Prevention and Atherosclerosis Research Centre, Robarts Research Institute, London, Ontario, Canada.

CHAPTER EIGHT
Doctors, Hospitals and Medicines

How to Protect Yourself From Your Doctor

The best doctors are sometimes the ones with the poorest personalities. Bedside manner is not necessarily a relevant criterion. *The prime dos and don'ts:*

•Do ask questions. Many patients are intimidated by the doctor's professional status. Don't be. Ask your prospective doctor about his medical philosophy. Pose specific questions—for example, does he believe in taking heroic measures in terminal cases? Look for a doctor who is attuned to the patient/doctor relationship. Be wary of a doctor who puts you off, who takes a question as a personal affront, or who says things like, "Don't worry, I'll take care of it."

•Don't be impressed by the diplomas on the wall. Many are probably from organizations that the doctor joined for a fee. *What you should know:* Is the doctor board-certified in his specialty?

•Do find out about the doctor's hospital affiliation. Is he on the medical staff of a hospital? Is it a local hospital of good reputation?

•Don't go straight to a specialist when you're having a problem. Specialists can be blind to any ailment that doesn't fall into their specialty. Have a generalist or internist assess your problem and send you to the appropriate specialist.

What Else to Consider

A doctor should be willing to reevaluate and reassess. Too many doctors are ready to write off a patient as neurotic. I've had any number of cases in which people judged neurotic had something physically wrong with them.

A patient has an absolute right to a second opinion. The mere fact that the doctor doesn't suggest it is no reason to assume you don't need one. Many doctors become unpleasant when a patient mentions getting a second opinion. Ignore that and get one anyway if you have any questions as to a doctor's evaluation or if surgery is recommended.

You have a right to your medical records. You'll need them for the second opinion. Most states have statutes that make it mandatory to give patients a copy (not the original) of their records.

Obstetric Malpractice

Since obstetrics is the most common area of malpractice today, there are certain points that pregnant women should be aware of:

•The doctor, not the nurse, should give the care. Nurses can take a blood pressure or pulse reading, but the doctor should do the internal examinations.

•Any woman in a high-risk group should get special attention. Women over 35 with their first baby need that special attention. So do women with a history of toxemia in the family and women with a cardiac, renal, or diabetic condition.

•Make sure your obstetrician does all the basics—asks a lot of questions, does regular urine tests, and pays attention to your weight and changes in uterine height. Special attention should be given to swelling, headaches, and post-term pregnancy.

Hospital Malpractice

In a hospital you can't interview everyone who will be giving you care. But there are some things you can do:

•Voice your complaints...and I don't mean about the tasteless food. Complain about things like an IV bottle that's been empty for an hour, or a catheter left in, or a doctor who says he'll be back in 10 minutes and instead returns the next day. Make friends with the nurses. Be polite but firm about what you need.

•Make sure the doctors and nurses know what you're allergic to. Be sure the allergies are adequately documented in the health records.

•Find out, especially in a teaching hospital, who is giving you care. Not everyone in a white coat is automatically qualified. You have a right to know how much training the doctor administering your treatment has received.

•Make sure you have given informed consent to any invasive procedure. The biggest issue in my office is patients who routinely sign anything that's put in front of them. Find out the risks and alternatives to any invasive procedure. Request an oral explanation in layman's terms. Make sure you totally understand anything you sign.

•Learn the names of the drugs you're getting. Find out what they're for and what their side effects are. Then, if someone hands you a drug you don't recognize, question it. If you're taking drugs from more than one doctor, be sure each knows what the other has prescribed, including over-the-counter medications.

•Ask the reason for each test you're given.

•Tell the doctor or nurse your full health history. Should malpractice occur, you won't have a leg to stand on in court if you've withheld vital information.

•Before you're discharged from the hospital, get full instructions about what you should do after you leave. Write down your questions about diet, bed rest, exercise, medication, or anything else that concerns you.

•If you believe that you have been injured by the hospital or the doctor, consult a lawyer who specializes in malpractice. Don't wait too long. There are different statutes of limitation in various jurisdictions.

Source: Leonard C. Arnold, MD, JD, Chicago.

How to Get Doctors to Talk to You on the Phone

It's generally very hard to find out whether a doctor treats your particular problem or uses the procedure you need until you visit the office —a waste of your time and money, since you'll probably have to wait for the appointment and pay for the visit.

Instead: Try to get the information on the telephone. *Obstacle:* Most office staffs tend to overprotect doctors from such calls—even, on occasion, contrary to the doctor's inclination.

Trick: Refer to yourself on the phone as "doctor." It's amazing how that can open doors with medical professionals. Not all people feel comfortable with such deception, but given the payoff, it should be considered.

Source: Susan G. Cole, editor of *The Practical Guide to Cancer Care*. Health Improvement Research Corp.

How to Get the Best From Your Doctor

Increasingly, patients are discovering they can no longer be passive in the doctor-patient relationship. They have to take an active interest to be sure they get not only the best care, but, in some instances, just adequate care—as the soaring number of medical malpractice suits seems to indicate.

Here is a valuable checklist of potential problems and advice for dealing with today's doctors…

•*Checkups:* The usual procedure is for a doctor to perform a physical checkup and do lab workups during the examination. Then, a few days later, the doctor's nurse calls and relates an oversimplified assessment of the lab results.

Instead: Arrange for a preliminary visit so that lab work can be done before the physical exam. That way, the doctor can go over the results of the tests in detail, answering any questions during the regular exam. If there is need for further lab work, it can be done later.

•*Medical records:* In most cases, your medical records are kept by the doctor. So if you move, decide to change doctors, or subsequently see a specialist, you have to go through a long procedure to get your records.

Instead: Ask for copies of all records and keep them in your own permanent file. *Especially useful:* Electrocardiograms, blood tests, and X rays. The doctor might charge you a nominal fee to make copies.

•*Doctor-patient relations:* Doctors usually prefer to be called "Doctor." Yet they frequently call patients by their first names.

That small difference helps to perpetuate the role of doctor as parent and patient as child— where the patient isn't expected to question the doctor's orders. This leaves the patient in a position of not sharing responsibility for his own health.

Instead: As a symbolic gesture, settle whether the two of you are on a first- or last-name basis.

More Ways to Win

•If the doctor always keeps you waiting, call before you leave for your appointment. *Even better:* Ask someone else to call and explain that your professional duties make your schedule very tight.

•If the doctor diagnoses an illness and prescribes drugs, take notes on the name of the condition and the drugs being prescribed.

•If you're overcome by the news of the illness (which isn't unusual), call the doctor after you've had some time to calm down and frame any questions about the prognosis and the method of treatment. Also, arrange to bring a relative or friend with you to emotionally-charged doctor visits.

That'll give you the emotional space to "collapse" or to go temporarily "deaf" to bad news, while your companion is able to listen, ask questions, and interpret what the doctor says. The period right after serious illness is disclosed is hard to handle, so make arrangements to compensate for it.

Drugs

Since even the "safest" drugs usually have some side effects, it's prudent to insist that you be included in any decisions about prescriptions.

Frequently, the decision isn't only which drug to take, but whether one should be taken at all. In some cases, there are alternatives to drugs... changes in diet, lifestyle, or exercise. Many doctors believe, perhaps correctly, that most patients don't feel that an office visit for an illness is complete unless a pill is prescribed. Make it clear that you don't feel that way.

•Insist that the druggist include the manufacturer's fact sheet with any prescription you're given. Read it. It's technical, but with the aid of a medical dictionary you may discover things about the drug you'll want to discuss with the doctor. It's hard, if not impossible, for doctors to know current information on all drugs. You may discover that the dose is excessive or that the medication is no longer considered effective for your condition.

•If you do take a drug that has side effects (dizziness, stomach distress, etc.), start taking it during a weekend or when you're home, so you'll be in a safer and more comfortable place when they hit.

Source: Susan G. Cole, editor of *The Practical Guide to Cancer Care*. Health Improvement Research Corp.

Doctors Do Not Eat Well

Most prefer red meat and chicken to fish... only 20% say they eat the recommended five servings of fruits and vegetables daily...and 55% are overweight.

Source: Nationwide study commissioned by Sudler & Hennessey, the health care and pharmaceuticals advertising division of Young & Rubicam, reported in *Adweek*, 1515 Broadway, New York 10036.

Fighting Premature Hospital Discharge

Patients are usually more than happy to leave the hospital following elective or emergency care. But some patients, mostly Medicare recipients, are being discharged before they've fully recovered.

Culprit: A pricing system established by Medicare that puts hospitals under pressure to discharge patients "quicker and sicker." Hospitals now have incentives to skimp on resources, and subtly devise ways to cut corners and increase their own profits. Medicare recipients include about 33 million people, mostly elderly.

You can fight an unjust early discharge. *Here's how:*

•Have your attending physician argue your case with the clinical director, who monitors length of stay. If the hospital still decides you must leave, appeal to your state's peer review organization, a government body that monitors hospital practices.

Although this may be a cumbersome process, the hospital will allow you a two-day grace period during the action. *Comforting:* Once you've begun an appeal process, chances are you will be allowed to stay longer. Hospitals know if a patient dies, they may face a malpractice suit.

•Contact the American Association of Retired Persons if you feel you've been mistreated. Few people realize the considerable power of this 28-million-member consumer organization. Write to the executive director of your local or regional chapter. The AARP can exert direct and indirect pressure on a hospital's chief executive officer.

The new pricing system resulted from Medicare's establishment of about 500 different groupings of inpatient and outpatient medical procedures, known as diagnostic related groups (DRGs).

Until five years ago, Medicare reimbursed a hospital for the cost of a procedure. Now Medicare uses DRGs to determine the average length of stay for a procedure and prices it accordingly. If the patient leaves before that "average period," the hospital makes money. If he stays longer, the hospital loses money. *Result:* Average length of stay in hospitals has dropped dramatically in the last few years.

On the positive side, DRGs have eliminated inefficiencies. Few patients need to stay longer than the designated period. Stays longer than necessary increase the chance of hospital-borne infections. However, no one should be discharged before it's medically wise.

Source: Uwe Reinhardt, PhD, James Madison professor of political economy, Woodrow Wilson School, Princeton University.

How to Get VIP Treatment In a Hospital

The first thing an admitting clerk does when you're brought into a hospital is slip a plastic tag with an identity number onto your wrist.

From that point on, like it or not, you are a number to most of the hospital staff.

Being a number instead of a name can be an awful shock. It means that you may be treated as if you have no identity—except for your symptoms, vital signs and medical treatment.

Fortunately, there are steps you can take to improve that treatment. And those steps, if successful, not only will make you feel more comfortable and human during your hospital visit, they could dramatically affect your state of health by the time you're ready to be discharged. In fact, it may be the issue that determines whether you leave alive or dead.

What You Can Do

Think of a hospital as a sort of huge, complex hotel—however, one that dispenses more than food, entertainment and lodging.

As you obviously know, a hospital dispenses both life-saving and life-threatening services. A moment's inattention at a hospital can lead to tragedy.

So how do you get the hospital to treat you like a person instead of a number?

In general, you've got to use the same techniques you use in other aspects of your personal and business life. The key word is assertiveness. That's not to say you should complain and be demanding—although, as you'll see, that may be necessary under certain circumstances.

Finding the Right Doctor

The first step in getting VIP treatment in a hospital should be taken long before you're admitted—and that's finding a doctor who can provide the leverage you'll need. You want someone with more than an M.D. after his name.

Every community has a clique of doctors who have "political" clout. Usually, these are physicians who serve on the local hospital's board of directors. Be aware, however, that a doctor with clout doesn't necessarily have the skills or any other attributes that make a physician a superior healer. Do you want such a person as your personal physician? Generally speaking, the answer is no, but there are exceptions. If you're satisfied that such a doctor can serve double-duty, so to speak, then you need go no farther.

The drawbacks:

Aside from the possibility that such a doctor may be more expert in a boardroom than an operating room there are other potential problems.

The most serious:

He may be more interested in keeping his professional calendar and the institution's beds

filled than in your welfare. Of course, there are ways to get around that. If he wants to admit you to the hospital for treatment and there is any doubt in your mind about this decision, ask for a consultation.

Generally speaking, it's always wise to get a consultation for any complex medical procedure—and the likelihood is that the procedure he's recommending is relatively complex if he wants to hospitalize you. So by asking for a consultation, you're not showing lack of faith in your doctor.

Caveat: However, we've heard of many instances where doctors are annoyed when a patient announces that he would like a consultation or second opinion. If you ever face a less-than-cooperative response to such a request, it would be prudent to seek out another doctor immediately. It's well within your rights to consult with as many physicians as you wish.

The Personal Touch

To guarantee better attention once you know that you're going to spend time in the hospital, make a date with the hospital administrator. He may or may not be a doctor—but in any case, he is a businessman, so you can be sure he speaks the same language as you. Introduce yourself. Tell him that you're a little concerned about your hospital stay and that you'd appreciate it if he'd take a personal interest in your case.

He'll get the message, and in all likelihood, he'll take steps to be sure that you're well cared for. Now that you've made your presence known, he will probably, out of courtesy, call the head of nursing and the admitting office and tell them you are coming to the hospital and that they should be expecting you. It's just such words, without pressure, that may make all the difference in the way you're subsequently treated.

Once You're in the Hospital

Even if you've failed or haven't had the time to take the above steps, there are still things you can do to ensure good treatment, if not VIP treatment.

If you're not physically up to it, your spouse or a friend or relative may have to help you, but if you're feeling well enough, you can take the following steps yourself.

•During the admission procedure, ask what rooms are available. You may prefer a private room, or for the sake of company, you may want to share a room with someone else. If you do want to share, ask about your potential partner's medical status to be sure that you can deal with his illness.

•After settling into your room, ask to see the dietitian. Explain that you understand that the hospital is not a hotel, but within reasonable bounds, and limited by doctor's orders, there are foods that you do and do not like. Itemize them. If you present your request with tact, the dietitian will probably try to meet your reasonable requests.

•Go out of your way to be polite to the nursing staff. They are your lifeline—literally. If the nurses take a dislike to you, the recuperation period will not be smooth.

•It's not tacky to provide small favors, such as a box of candy, and even flowers, on each of the three nursing shifts: the 8 am to 4 pm, the 4 pm to midnight, and midnight to 8 am. Don't offer a gratuity until you're ready to be discharged. Nurses are professionals, and most would resent the offer. But if you received extra special care from a nurse during your stay, a tasteful gift isn't inappropriate.

•Make it clear that you'd like to know what medication or treatment is being given to you beforehand. That will require a discussion with your doctor. Most doctors work on the premise that patients don't want to know too much, and so only provide information as it's necessary or if the patient specifically requests it.

Why you should want this information:

Unfortunately, mistakes are made now and then, but if you ask the nurse, "What are these pills?" or, "What exactly will you be doing to me?", and she has orders from your doctor to provide that information on request, then it gives the staff the opportunity to double-check what they are doing and it gives you a chance to say, "Wait a minute!" if an obvious error is being committed.

How to Complain

If you're not happy with your care, explain your complaint firmly and politely to the nurse. If that gets you no place, ask to speak to the head nurse. And if that fails, you may have to speak to either your doctor or the hospital administrator. Usually, when you reach that level, and you're not being unreasonable, steps will be taken to satisfy your complaint and resolve your problem.

Getting Fast Emergency Medical Care

Inside information: If you arrive at a hospital by ambulance, you usually will receive a higher priority…even if you could have gotten to the hospital without the ambulance. If your condition is serious enough that taking an ambulance isn't frivolous, it's a good strategy to call one. *Best:* Arriving in the hospital's own ambulance, because you automatically become one of the hospital's patients…and its patients receive priority.

For the same reason, the ambulance of a local volunteer unit or fire district is a good choice. These people know the local ER personnel, and they are your neighbors. *Recommended:* Contribute to their fund drives and post your contribution stickers.

If your condition is very serious: Call the police —always dial 911. Police response with an ambulance—or transport by the police themselves, if no ambulance is available—will help facilitate matters at the hospital. *Helpful:* Call the ambulance a "bus"—the inside term used by police. *Aim:* To get them to assume that you or a close relative is a cop and render service accordingly.

Source: Harry Alberts, MSW, certified social worker, Box 402, Commack, NY 11725. Mr. Alberts was formerly with the New York State Department of Health.

The Taoist Principals of Preventive Medicine

Many Chinese follow a way of life called *Taoism.* Its goals are to promote balance and harmony…in both the immediate environment and the universe. Taoists believe that anyone can reach a state of enlightenment called *hsing ming shuang hsiu,* the balance of mind and body. *Required:* Great self-discipline and personal effort, including the cultivation of health and longevity.

Interesting: The Taoist emphasis on preventive medicine is so strong that in old China people paid their physician only when they were well. If they got sick, the treatment was free.

The Breath of Life

Taoists believe in an internal energy called *Chi,* the breath of life. Chi corresponds closely to western concepts of bioelectricity, the body's electrical program. By changing this inner program, people can influence their metabolism in a way that actually strengthens the immune system.

Taoists believe that Chi flows through a system of subtle veins, called meridians. If the Chi is blocked anywhere in the body, you'll have too much Chi—too much energy—on one side of the blockage, and too little on the other.

To open the blocked areas along the meridians so the Chi can flow freely, the Chinese use a series of exercises that involve breathing, gentle movement and visualization.

Called *Chi kung*, these exercises are based on five animals—the crane, bear, monkey, deer, and tiger. Each exercise affects a specific internal organ and bodily system. Chi kung, which resemble tai chi exercises, are easy to learn.

The Three Treasures

In addition to the meridian system, Taoists believe that the human body contains three basic forms of energy that create health when they are in balance with each other.

•*Chi* is breath energy. It resides in the chest and lungs.

The three sources of Chi are the air we breathe, the food we eat, and the energy and strength of the immune system that we inherit from our parents. The more Chi you accumulate, the greater your vitality and better your health.

Exercise: Stand with your feet about shoulder-width apart, legs slightly bent, back straight but not stiff, chest relaxed, abdomen loose, with your palms at waist height, facing downward. Inhale and allow the lower abdomen and back to expand as though you were filling a balloon. When you exhale, the lower abdomen and back should contract. Continue to do this exercise as long as you can comfortably. If there's pain there's no gain.

This exercises the diaphragm, gently massaging the internal organs. And because the lower lobes of the lungs are stretched downward, the body can take in more air…and more Chi.

•*Jing* is sexual energy, which is believed to be stored in the lower abdomen and cultivated through balanced sexual relationships.

Exercise: To enhance Jing, stimulate the endocrine system, and improve sexual health, men should contract the muscles of the perineum (the soft band of muscles located between the scrotum and anus) when they inhale and release when they exhale. Women should contract and release the anal and vaginal muscles while continuing to breathe naturally. These exercises, known in the West as Kegel exercises, also help solve sexual problems, including prostate enlargement in men and irregular menstruation in women.

•*Shen* is spiritual or intuitive energy. Shen, which means clarity of mind, requires the ability to temporarily shut off the interference of constant thinking. Most people's minds are like a TV that they can't turn off. Without the clarity and fullness of Shen, which is developed through meditation, none of the other techniques are possible.

Exercise: Sit upright in a chair and breathe at a natural pace. At the same time, observe any thoughts that pass by, as if you were watching passing clouds. Make no judgments and don't try to control or manipulate your thoughts. I call this being an open window of awareness. And although it may sound quite easy, it is very difficult for most westerners, who always have to be doing something.

Basic Taoist Principles

There are two underlying principles of Taoist philosophy that tell us how to live in a manner that promotes health and well-being.

•*Tzu jan* involves things that grow from the inside out rather than being created outside. *Translation:* Spontaneity, which shouldn't be confused with impulsiveness. Spontaneity means sensing what is coming from inside you and allowing it to express itself.

•*Wu wei,* or effortlessness, involves going with the flow, lacking artifice, using only those muscles needed for the task at hand.

Taoists think that these two principles should be applied consistently on every level—lifestyle, relationships, exercise, movement, etc.

Example: Unless sexual partners surrender completely to the experience, there can be no exchange of energy. *Result:* None of the elaborate Taoist sex techniques will work until both partners are willing to go with the flow of the experience and express whatever they feel.

Source: Kenneth S. Cohen, MA in psychology, a master scholar of Chinese healing arts. A former faculty member of Boulder Graduate School psychology department, he is currently director of the Taoist Mountain Retreat in Nederland, CO.

Drugs that Work Best when Taken on an Empty Stomach

Food slows the absorption of certain drugs, so they are best taken without food. If nausea or stomach upset results, discuss it with your physician or pharmacist. Common drugs that fall into this category include:

•Acetaminophen* (Tylenol, etc.)

•Enteric-coated aspirin

•Ampicillin

•Erythromycin

•Epsom salts

•Levodopa

•Mineral oil

•Magnesium hydroxide (milk of magnesia)

*Generic names are given.

•Penicillin G and V

•Tetracycline

•Procainamide

Source: *50+: The Graedon's People's Pharmacy for Older Adults* by Joe and Teresa Graedon. Bantam Books.

Retin-A—Will it Make Skin Look Younger?

Retin-A can rectify, and may even prevent, the effects of chronic sun exposure on your skin—roughness, loss of elasticity, coarseness, brown spots, sallowness, precancerous lesions, blackheads around the eyes, etc.

Retin-A cannot, however, prevent the effects of the normal aging process, which are usually less severe than those caused by the sun and include roughness, laxity, and benign tumors.

It can:

•Improve skin color by increasing blood flow. Photoaging, which decreases blood flow, causes skin to become yellowish. As Retin-A increases blood flow, the complexion turns rosy again.

•Restore elasticity by boosting collagen production, which is usually retarded by photoaging.

•Thicken the epidermis by increasing cell turnover, which is also slowed by photoaging, and by stimulating the growth of the tiny blood vessels in the skin.

•Eliminate blotchiness and sun spots by improving the distribution of melanosomes (pigment granules) in the skin.

•Produce smoother, non-scaly skin by accelerating the shedding of the outer layer of dead cells. *Also:* The skin cells underneath, which then push their way to the surface, are more normal and look better than photoaged cells. *Result:* A smooth, more even skin color and texture.

•Correct sun-induced DNA damage by regulating abnormal cell reproduction. *Also:* Retin-A could lessen risk of skin cancer, but this hasn't been proven yet. Preliminary evidence shows that it reduces actinic keratoses—precancerous lesions.

None of the vitamin A products sold over-the-counter produce the same results as Retin-A. Although some of them may end up being converted to vitamin A acid in the skin, the effect is not significant.

Source: Dr. Alan Shalita, chairman, department of dermatology, State University of New York Health Science Center, Brooklyn.

Advantages of Buying Drugs Overseas

Many drugs that require a prescription in the US are sold over the counter in other countries. *Example:* Cough syrup with codeine.

Even when a medication requires a prescription overseas, most foreign doctors will give you one if you say you have a prescription in the US.

Prescription drugs that are commonly sold over the counter outside the US:

•Amoxicillin antibiotic

•Digoxin cardiac regulator

•Erythromycin antibiotic

•Lasix diuretic

•Metronidazole antifungal

•Penicillin antibiotic

•Prednisone steroid

•Propranolol cardiac regulator

Rules about prescriptions are much looser overseas. In Latin America, for instance, doctors commonly write large-quantity (100 tablets plus), refillable prescriptions for drugs that in the US require a new prescription each time the drug is dispensed.

Outside the US you can buy some medications that aren't available here, even with a prescription.

Also more readily available overseas: Experimental drugs.

Many people who suffer from fatal and very serious diseases are turned down for experimental treatment in the US. *Reasons:* There are manufacturers' restrictions on which patients are eligible for experimentation and there is potential for enormous losses from lawsuits.

The risks: Side effects and proper dosages of experimental medications aren't fully known. That's one of the reasons the Food and Drug Administration hasn't approved them for general use.

Source: Cynthia Ronan, MD, a pharmacologist at Griffin Hospital, 130 Division St., Derby, CT 06718.

How to Protect Yourself Against Disease-Mongering

When it comes to treating cancer, heart disease, severe trauma, and other life-threatening ailments, the American health-care system is second to none. Our doctors are highly trained, our drugs carefully screened, our hospitals chockablock with sophisticated medical equipment.

Still, it pays to remember that a desire to aid the afflicted isn't the only motive driving our health-care system. *Also at work:* A powerful and unrelenting urge to maximize profits.

In order to remain in business, doctors, hospitals, diagnostic facilities, drug and medical equipment makers, insurance companies and other recipients of our health-care dollars all need one thing—patients with health insurance. The greater their number, the sicker they are, the more drugs they take, the more tests they undergo… the bigger the industry's profits.

Problem: To get more patients, the health-care industry often resorts to an insidious form of exploitation known as disease-mongering.

Disease-mongering takes many forms…

•It's the surgeon who insists upon treating a minor heart ailment with costly and often risky bypass surgery—just to earn more money.

•It's the drug maker that uses manipulative ads to portray the common cold as a debilitating ailment in need of drug therapy.

•It's the diagnostic clinic that sells mammograms even to women for whom there's no evidence that they work.

•It's also the medical journalist who earns his keep by hyping minor illnesses as plagues.

No matter what form disease-mongering takes, however, the result never varies—healthy people are led to believe they're ill or at risk of becoming ill…and persons suffering from minor ailments are led to believe they're seriously ill.

The health-care industry knows that once we're instilled with fear, we'll take action—scheduling costly medical checkups and diagnostic tests at the merest hint of trouble…using cold remedies, painkillers, and other drugs for conditions that clear up even without treatment… gobbling prescription drugs with nasty and potentially harmful side effects…and submitting to surgery that is risky and of questionable benefit.

Watch Out for…

•Manipulative ads. Television, newspapers, and magazines are filled with ads for sinus remedies, arthritis pills, headache relievers—and, of course, even baldness cures.

The more often we encounter these ads, the more firmly we're convinced that we need the products they promote. *Reality:* Minor aches and pains, as well as occasional cold or flu symptoms, are a normal part of life. There's no good reason to visit the drugstore every time you sneeze.

To avoid being manipulated:

Each time you choose to read a health ad, ask yourself who really stands to benefit from its message—you or the makers of the product. Are there alternatives? What would happen if you took no action? Use only those products truly beneficial to you.

•"Man-made" diseases. While there's no doubt that broken bones and heart attacks need prompt treatment, not all medical conditions require treatment.

Example: Mild hypertension. The cutoff between "normal" and "high" blood pressure has been set arbitrarily low in this country—as a result, inflating the ranks of the "ill" and maximizing the profit potential for doctors and companies selling antihypertensive drugs. In fact, a blood pressure reading treated in this country with an aggressive drug regimen might be considered normal in England.

Blood pressure isn't the only such "manmade" disease. Elevated cholesterol level is considered a heart-disease risk factor—and rightly so. But often even mildly elevated cholesterol is treated as a disease in its own right. *Result:* People who feel perfectly fine are urged to take harsh and costly drugs, even though evidence of their value is controversial.

And in an effort to sell more estrogen, drug makers are now trying to turn menopause from a natural process into a deficiency disease that needs treatment. The list goes on and on.

To avoid trouble: If a doctor says you're at risk for or already have a particular disease and urges aggressive treatment, follow the advice only if there's solid evidence that the treatment will cut your risk. Get a second opinion, and do your own research.

•Needless diagnostic tests. Doctors order far too many diagnostic tests. Each time you have a mammogram, stress test, cholesterol test, AIDS test, etc., you're taking a risk. Not only that you'll hear bad news, but your test results could be wrong. The test might indicate you're okay when you're really sick, for instance, or that you're sick when you're healthy.

Danger: A "false positive" causes not only needless anxiety, but also labels you as "sick" and thereby jeopardizes your insurability. It can even lead you to seek risky treatments.

Example: There have been cases in which people died during heart surgery scheduled after stress tests mistakenly indicated that they had heart disease.

To avoid trouble: For anyone already at reasonably high risk for a particular condition, the potential benefits of being tested generally outweigh the risk of inaccurate results. But if your risk for the ailment is very low, avoid being tested. Ask your doctor to explain your level of risk when making the decision.

Make sure the doctors with whom you discuss your case have no financial stake in performing the test.

Scandalous: Though the conflict of interest in such an arrangement is obvious, many doctors now own their own CT scanners, MRI scanners, and other diagnostic equipment. The more tests they schedule, the more money they make.

•Free screening clinics. These days, free screening is being offered for everything from prostate cancer to high blood pressure. It sounds like a good idea. But in many cases these clinics are set up to bring in more patients…and are more beneficial to their sponsors than to the general public.

Problem: Unreliable readings. Some serious medical problems are missed entirely, while problems are diagnosed in persons who are actually perfectly healthy.

To avoid trouble: Be tested in a doctor's office or a diagnostic facility specializing in medical tests. Make sure the person who interprets the test results is highly experienced.

•Needless surgery. A surprisingly large percentage of operations in this country are performed needlessly—up to 25% by some respectable estimates. Certain procedures are especially likely to be performed inappropriately, including hysterectomy, back surgery, Cesarean sections, and bypass surgery. *Result:* Needless expense, discomfort, and even the risk of fatal complications —all because a surgeon was eager to operate.

To avoid trouble: Always get a second opinion before agreeing to surgery. Many problems frequently treated with surgery can be resolved more cheaply and safely via exercise, changes in diet, physical therapy, and other nonsurgical methods.

•Overbearing doctors. Americans tend to be much more deferential toward doctors than toward lawyers, accountants, and other professionals we employ—and doctors rarely do anything to stop us.

Explanation: Most of us started seeing doctors when we were kids, and we still behave like kids in the presence of them.

Better way: Instead of blindly accepting your doctor's advice, make it a point to discuss all your available options.

Helpful: Calling your doctor by his/her first name—especially if the doctor calls you by yours. Doing so reminds you that you're on an equal footing with one another—that you're hiring the doctor, not the other way around.

•Overly aggressive treatment. Every good doctor knows that too much medical care is just as deleterious as too little. Unfortunately, patients often demand aggressive treatment.

Problem: While such treatment might be warranted for serious ailments, most conditions do just as well with minimal or no treatment. In fact, few medical conditions call for urgent intervention of any kind.

Certainly you should see a doctor right away for obvious injuries, severe pain, or high fever. In many cases, however, it's not only safe to wait a few weeks before seeking medical care, it's the smartest course of action.

Reason: Many conditions improve or disappear without treatment, saving you money, aggravation and more.

Source: Lynn Payer, former editor of *The New York Times Good Health Magazine* and author of several books on medical topics, including *Disease-Mongers: How Doctors, Drug Companies, and Insurers Are Making You Feel Sick.* John Wiley & Sons.

CHAPTER NINE
Diet and Nutrition

The Minerals in Our Food

Thanks to everything we've read and heard lately about fat, fiber, and food additives, we've all become much smarter about what we're eating—and that's great.

However—a surprising number of myths remain concerning the minerals we take in, both in our daily diets and in the form of supplements. And that misinformation can be dangerous... even deadly.

What we do know for certain is that minerals are essential for life. To a large extent, the body is composed of minerals. For example, our blood carries significant amounts of sodium, potassium, and chloride. And our bones and teeth are rich in calcium, phosphorous, and magnesium.

The news about minerals is generally good: If you eat a healthy, varied diet—including adequate amounts of milk, fruits, and vegetables—your body should get all the minerals it requires. Special needs do arise, however.

Example: As people age, calcium is less well utilized, and extra amounts are recommended, especially for women. Prolonged gastrointestinal illness, and certain drugs, may also change requirements.

Minerals are an often-misunderstood category of nutrients, and you may do well to let go of some of the myths:

•*Myth:* A salty taste is a reliable indicator of salt content.

Truth: Food-content labels must be read very carefully—some items that you would never suspect to be high in sodium are. For example, ounce for ounce, certain dry cereals contain more salt than potato chips.

As most of us now know, too much salt in the diet can promote high blood pressure—and possibly strokes in susceptible individuals. We require only a tiny amount of salt to maintain good health—just 500 milligrams daily, or the equivalent of a quarter-teaspoon. Chances are you're getting more than that amount naturally from the foods you eat each day—you need never go near a salt shaker. In fact, the average American consumes closer to 4,000 to 5,000 milligrams per day—10 times what's needed, and in some ethnic groups, it can be twice that amount.

If you're a salt-lover, you'd be wise to wean yourself off it. Our taste for salt (or any other flavor) is acquired and thus can be unlearned at any age.

To keep your kids from getting hooked on salt, don't serve them salty food or snacks.

•*Myth:* Calcium deficiency is really only of concern to women approaching menopause.

Truth: Women are never too young to step up their calcium intake to help ward off future osteoporosis. Even teenage girls should start taking calcium supplements to build bone strength, especially if they don't drink milk. Bones that are strong at an early age are less likely to leach out calcium, a process that leads to fractures and other problems later on.

Between the ages of 19 and 24, women (and men) should be sure to get 1,200 milligrams of calcium per day—the amount provided by approximately a quart of milk. If you know you're not taking in sufficient quantities of calcium from your food—and most people's diets are imperfect—by all means take a calcium supplement.

•*Myth:* "Health" foods are better sources of minerals than ordinary foods.

Truth: Some so-called "health" or "natural" foods can in fact be harmful.

Example: Health-food fans will often buy "natural" calcium supplements. These supplements are generally produced from limestone and are rich in calcium and magnesium, but they can also contain dangerous impurities, including lead.

In general, it's unwise to buy foods that haven't been carefully inspected and analyzed by government agencies. *Problem:* Many products found in health-food stores have not undergone rigorous inspection. If you choose a food or a supplement that hasn't been government-approved, you run the risk of ingesting impurities. While some of them are harmless, others are not.

•*Myth:* Minerals lost through sweat during strenuous exercise should be replaced via a mineral-rich drink such as Gatorade or by taking salt tablets.

Truth: Gatorade, a dilute solution of some of the minerals found in the body, is a perfectly fine product, but you rarely need it. Your body will restore its lost minerals on its own.

It's far more important to replenish the water your body has lost in sweat.

As for salt tablets, athletes used to rely on them, but nowadays we know that these tablets can do more harm than good. Again, it's best to stick to plain water after your workout, unless the salt loss was truly excessive.

Exception: Pedialyte is a solution that pediatricians may give to children who've become dehydrated from excessive vomiting or diarrhea. That's because youngsters have a much more delicate constitution than adults, and so their water and mineral levels must be restored quickly and completely.

Minimum Daily Requirements

•Sodium. 500 mg. (¼ teaspoon of table salt). *Sodium-rich foods:* Those that have been pickled, canned, smoked, or cured...soy sauce...luncheon meats...salted snack foods.

•Potassium. 2,000 mg. *Some potassium-rich foods include:* Bananas (four)...orange juice (four 8-ounce glasses)...carrots (six).

•Chloride. 750 mg. (or ¼ teaspoon of table salt). *Chloride-rich foods:* Most processed foods.

•Calcium. 1,200 mg. (ages 19 to 24)...800 mg. (age 25 and over). *Some calcium-rich foods:* Milk (three 8-ounce glasses)...plain yogurt (three 8-ounce cups)...cheddar cheese (6 ounces).

•Phosphorus. 1,200 mg. (ages 19 to 24)...800 mg. (age 25 and over). *Phosphorus-rich foods:* Same as those rich in calcium.

•Magnesium. 350 mg. (men), 280 mg. (women). *Some magnesium-rich foods:* Green beans (five cups)...Brazil nuts (12).

•Sulfur. A daily requirement has not been established. *Sulfur-rich foods:* Cheese, eggs, milk, meat, nuts, vegetables.

Some essential trace elements—needed by the body in miniscule amounts...

•Iron. *Daily requirement:* 10 mg. (men)...15 mg. (women ages 19 to 50)...10 mg. (women 51 and over). *Some iron-rich foods:* Liver (4 ounces)...breakfast cereal, such as Cheerios or Raisin Bran (2 ounces).

•Selenium. *Daily requirement:* 70 micrograms (men)...55 micrograms (women). *Some selenium-rich foods:* Canned tuna (2½ ounces)...molasses (2 ounces).

•Iodine. *Daily requirement:* 150 micrograms. *Some iodine-rich foods:* Iodized salt...haddock (4 ounces)...milk (8 ounces)...plain yogurt (two 8-ounce cups).

Source: Mia Parsonnet, MD, a member of the clinical faculty of the New Jersey College of Medicine and Dentistry. She is author of *What's Really in Our Food? Fact and Fiction about Fat and Fiber, Vitamins and Minerals, Nutrients, and Contaminants.* Shapolsky Publishers, Inc.

Seafood Savvy

Seafood and fish are an excellent protein source that is low in saturated fat, light on calories, and high in vitamins, minerals, and the omega-3 fatty acids that help reduce the risk of heart disease.

But there are risks. More than 80% of the seafood eaten in the US has not been inspected for chemical or microbial contaminants. Fortunately, there are things that you can do to enjoy maximum health and minimum risk...

•Avoid chemical contaminants. When you buy fish, choose younger, smaller ones, since they've accumulated fewer contaminants. Low-fat, offshore species like cod, haddock, and pollack are especially good choices. Always trim the skin, belly flap, and dark meat along the top or center, especially when it comes to fatty fish such as bluefish. Don't use the fatty parts to make sauce. Don't eat the green "tomalley" in lobsters or the "mustard" in crabs.

•Avoid natural toxins. When traveling in tropical climates, avoid reef fish such as amberjack, grouper, goatfish, or barracuda, which are more likely to be contaminated. Buy only seafood that has been kept continuously chilled, especially mahi-mahi, tuna, and bluefish, which produce an odorless toxin when they spoil.

•Avoid disease-causing microbes. Bite for bite, raw or undercooked shellfish is the riskiest food you can eat.

Self-defense: Don't eat shellfish whose shells remain closed after cooking. Do not eat raw fish or shellfish if you are over 60, HIV-positive, pregnant, have cancer or liver disease, or are vulnerable to infection. Cook all fish and shellfish thoroughly. Raw clams, oysters, and mussels should be steamed for six minutes.

•Don't buy fresh fish that has dull, sunken eyes, or fish that smells "fishy." Do not buy ready-to-eat seafood that is displayed too close to raw seafood.

Source: Lisa Y. Lefferts, an environmental-health consultant in Hyattsville, Maryland, who specializes in food safety, environmental policy, and risk assessment.

Hot-Flash Prevention

Japanese women have fewer hot flashes and other menopausal symptoms than American women. *Possible reason:* They eat about two ounces a day of foods made from soybeans, such as tofu (bean curd) and miso (soybean paste). Soybeans are rich in isoflavinoids, which are converted during digestion to estrogen-like substances that can help prevent hot flashes.

Sources: Barry Goldin, PhD, and Sherwood Gorbach, MD, Tufts University School of Medicine, and Herman Adlercreutz, MD, Helsinki University, Finland.

How You Cook Has a Lot to Do With Fiber Content

How much fiber a food gives you depends considerably on the method of preparation. Leaving the skins on vegetables and fruits enhances their fiber content. Browning bread increases its fiber (which is why crusts have more fiber than the interior of a loaf). Stir-frying or sautéing vegetables adds fiber more than boiling because less soluble fiber is removed. Deep-frying increases fiber, too, but at great cost in fat and calories. On the other hand, puréeing food decreases fiber, and reducing foods to juice almost completely destroys fiber content.

What to Eat to Prevent Cancer... And What Not to Eat

Although scientists continue to debate the role specific foods play in the development of cancer, there's now a consensus that Americans could dramatically lower their cancer risk by altering their eating habits—specifically, by eating less fat and more fiber.

The Fat Connection

Most Americans consume 38% to 40% of their total calories in the form of fat—well above the 25% to 30% fat consumption considered desirable.

This makes us highly susceptible to cancer of the colon, breast, pancreas, and prostate.

No one knows exactly why eating too much fat promotes the development of cancer, but the evidence—drawn from studies on both animals and humans—is compelling.

Different foods contain different types and quantities of fat...

•Saturated fats are found in beef and other meats, fried foods, and poultry skin.

•Monounsaturated fats are found in peanuts, olives and a few other foods.

•Polyunsaturated fats are found in corn, safflower, and other cooking oils.

•Very unsaturated long-chain fatty acids are found in cold-water fish, such as herring and salmon.

It's important to keep track of what kinds of fats you eat because nutritionists now recommend that these fats be eaten in a 1:1:1 ratio. In other words, each day we should eat equal portions of polyunsaturated, monounsaturated, and saturated fats. For most of us, this means cutting down on saturated fats while increasing intake of monounsaturated and polyunsaturated fats.

To reduce your consumption of saturated fats, eat less fried foods, trim the fat off beef and other meats, and trim skin off poultry. These small sacrifices have big health payoffs.

About fish: Although fish contains oils that are highly unsaturated, it's still unclear what, if any, role this oil plays in preventing cancer. There is some early evidence, however, that eating large amounts of fish reduces cancer risk and lowers serum triglycerides—lipids that may be associated with heart disease.

The Fiber Connection

While we're eating too much fat, we're also eating too little fiber. On the average, Americans consume only 10 to 12 grams of fiber a day. Instead, we should be eating 25 to 30 grams of fiber every day. (One gram is equivalent in weight to three pennies.)

Big problem: Our diet consists of highly refined, easy-to-chew foods instead of high-fiber fruits, vegetables, and grains.

There are two basic kinds of fiber:

•Insoluble fiber, found primarily in wheat bran, is fiber that is not broken down by bacteria in the intestine. By helping waste pass quickly through the colon, it helps prevent colon cancer, diverticulitis, and appendicitis.

•Soluble fiber, found in oat bran and in most fruits and vegetables, is fiber that is broken down by bacteria. It helps to prevent heart disease (by lowering cholesterol) and diabetes (by lowering the blood sugar).

Nutritionists now recommend that Americans should double their intake of dietary fiber... fruits and vegetables as well as grains. Pears, for instance, at 4.6 grams of fiber each, contain more fiber than any other fruit. *Other good fiber sources:* Red kidney beans (7 grams), lentils (4 grams), apples (3.3 grams), bananas (2.7 grams), and grapefruit (1.5 grams per half).

Caution: Don't consume more than 40 grams of fiber a day. Too much can be almost as bad as too little. In animals, excessive consumption has been found to cause bulky stools that can result in a form of constipation.

There also is some early evidence that alfalfa and certain other grains may actually increase the risk of developing colon cancer. *Self-defense:* Until the final verdict is in, don't rely just on grains for your fiber...eat a wide variety of fiber-rich foods.

Beyond Fat and Fiber

Other than increasing fiber and reducing fats, evidence linking dietary choices to cancer is less reliable.

Still, there are things to do that probably will help prevent cancer...and which won't hurt in any case.

•Eat a wide variety of foods. This limits your exposure to any carcinogens that might be found in a particular food...and eliminates the need for vitamin and mineral supplements.

•Increase your consumption of vitamin A. A powerful antioxidant, it keeps our cells from being attacked by oxygen, and thus prevents cancer. Vitamin A seems particularly effective in helping prevent lung cancer in smokers. To a lesser extent, it also seems to help stave off colon cancer, breast cancer, and lung cancer. *Best vitamin A sources:* Carrots, squash, and other orange and leafy vegetables.

•Increase your intake of selenium. Selenium is a trace element found in most vegetables. To get more into your diet, eat more vegetables. *Alternative:* Selenium supplements.

•Limit your consumption of smoked and pickled foods. They have been tied to stomach cancer. An occasional dill pickle won't hurt you, and neither will an occasional barbecued meal. But a daily regimen of pickled vegetables and smoked meats is imprudent.

•Avoid obesity. Obesity is clearly linked to cancer of both the endometrium (the lining of the uterus) and the breast. Also, obese women with breast cancer are far more likely to succumb to the disease than are normal-weight women diagnosed with similar breast cancer.

Keeping track of your diet is one step toward controlling your weight. *Also extremely helpful:* Exercise.

Watching TV, working in an office, and other aspects of a sedentary lifestyle all are associated with cancer.

Although it's not yet clear exactly how exercise helps prevent cancer, the incidence of colon cancer is much higher in men with sedentary occupations than men who are active. Women athletes have lower rates of reproductive-tract cancer than sedentary, out-of-shape women. And animal studies have demonstrated that moderate exercise cuts the risk of breast, pancreas, liver, and colon cancer.

Caution: Too much exercise may actually be almost as bad as too little. Several studies have indicated that extreme exertion (like that necessary to complete a marathon) temporarily weakens the immune system, opening the way for infectious bacteria and viruses—and possibly the development of cancer.

Evidence: At the turn of the century, stomach cancer was common in the US. Now that refrigeration is almost universal—and we rely less on pickling and smoking to preserve our foods—it is a rarity. In Japan, however, where pickled and smoked foods remain common, stomach cancer rates are among the highest in the world.

•Limit your consumption of simple carbohydrates (sugars). Evolving man ate very little sugar. As a result of this, our bodies are not set up to properly digest it.

Problem: Simple carbohydrates cause the pancreas to produce a large amount of insulin very rapidly, and there is now some evidence suggesting that this can have a harmful effect on the pancreas. *Better:* Complex carbohydrates—found in pastas and breads.

•Limit your caffeine consumption. Caffeine has been tied to a variety of cancers, including those of the pancreas and bladder. More recent data suggest caffeine does not cause cancer. Nonetheless, caffeine is very clearly a potent drug, and it makes sense to consume it in moderation.

•Limit your alcohol consumption. Drinking to excess (more than a couple of drinks a day) has been linked to cancer of the mouth and throat. People who drink and smoke are at high risk. Most patients with head or neck cancer are alcoholics or near-alcoholics with poor nutritional habits who smoke regularly.

Source: Leonard A. Cohen, PhD, head of the section of nutritional endocrinology, the American Health Foundation, One Dana Rd., Valhalla, NY 10595. Dr. Cohen's specialty is in the area of nutritional carcinogenesis.

Calcium vs. Memory

Memory impairment may be caused by too much calcium. Calcium is involved in the transmission of messages along brain neurons in the portion of the brain thought to direct memory functions.

As rats age, calcium flow into nerve cells increases, impairing the flow of messages. *Implications:* If similar results occur in humans, calcium-blocking drugs might be used to prevent memory loss...calcium supplements may contribute to memory loss.

Source: Philip Landfield, MD, professor of physiology, Bowman Gray School of Medicine, Wake Forest University, Winston-Salem, NC.

The Fiber/Calcium Connection

Dietary fiber can prevent the body from absorbing calcium. *Recommended:* Eat high-fiber and high-calcium foods at different times.

Source: *American Health,* New York.

CHAPTER TEN

Fitness and Exercise

Exercise and Your Immune System

Brisk walks strengthen your immune system —but too-strenuous workouts can lower immunity to colds and flu. Exercising near your maximum capacity for just 45 minutes—or more— produces a six-hour "window" of vulnerability afterward. *Better:* Exercise at a moderate level— the equivalent of a brisk walk—if not training for competition.

Source: David Nieman, DrPH, professor of health, department of health and exercise science, Appalachian State University, Boone, NC.

Improved Backswings For Older Golfers

Backswings get shorter as golfers get older. When the swing gets too short, you'll lose distance, accuracy, and consistency.

Remedies: Hold the club lightly. *Reason:* Too tight a grip tenses the arm and shoulder muscles and restricts the backswing.

Put more weight on your right foot, especially on full swings with woods and longer irons. *Result:* A head start on your swing and less weight to shift.

Turn your chin to the right (or to the left, if you're a southpaw) as you start your backswing. If it throws your timing off, cock your chin in the direction of the backswing before you swing.

Exercises to Do In the Car

(1) *Double chin:* Lift chin slightly and open and close mouth as though chewing. (2) *Flabby neck:* Move head toward right shoulder while looking straight ahead at the road. Return head to center, then toward left shoulder. (3) *Pot belly:* Sit straight with spine against back seat. Pull stomach in and hold breath for count of 5. Relax, then repeat. The exercise also relieves tension and helps fight sleepiness.

Spotting Fraudulent Weight-Loss Programs

Avoid weight-loss programs that:
•Promise rapid weight loss (substantially more than 1% of total body weight per week).

•Try to make clients dependent on special products rather than teaching how to make good choices from conventional foods.

•Do not encourage permanent, realistic life-style changes.

•Misrepresent salespeople as "counselors" supposedly qualified to give guidance in nutrition and/or general health.

•Require a large sum of money at the start, or require clients to sign a contract for an expensive, long-term program.

•Fail to inform clients about the various health risks associated with weight loss.

•Promote unproven or spurious weight-loss aids.

•Claim that "cellulite" exists in the body.

•Claim that the use of an appetite suppressant or bulking agent enables a person to lose fat without restricting caloric intake.

•Claim that a weight-control product contains a unique ingredient or component, unless that component really is not available in other weight-loss products.

Source: William T. Jarvis, PhD, president of the National Council Against Health Fraud, quoted in *Nutrition Forum*, George F. Stickley Co., Philadelphia 19106.

How Men Can Lose 10 to 75 Pounds...for Good

From everything we read and hear, it may seem as though weight were primarily a woman's problem.

In fact, there are more overweight men than overweight women. There are now approximately 25 million men in the United States who are considered clinically obese (more than 20% above their ideal weight).

And there are another 10 to 15 million men who are heavier than they would like to be. For men, weight-gain frequently accompanies middle age and a higher-than-average socioeconomic status.

Four Basic Steps

• Control stress-eating. Uncontrolled, unplanned nibbling tends to involve high-fat, snack-type foods.

If you find yourself eating from stress or other emotions, such as anger or frustration, seek out enjoyable alternatives, which can include reading a mystery or going out to a movie.

If you're at your job, try to leave the building for a 10-minute walk or do some deep breathing while sitting at your desk.

• Avoid alcohol. Alcohol is high in calories and impairs judgment. In addition, it tends to work against your self-restraint when you're eating out.

Example: Drinking a glass or two of wine before ordering an entrée can lower your guard when the waiter shows up. Alcohol improves the chances that you'll switch from the plain green salad and broiled fish you intended to order to prime rib and salad drenched in bleu-cheese dressing. Further, alcohol in the system slows down the body's fat-burning process.

• Decrease the amount of fat you consume. This one basic nutritional change can make a big difference in your weight.

Reduce dietary fat, found in red meat, fried and greasy foods, cheese, chips and ice cream, to name but a few. You'll lose weight even if you eat the same quantity of food as before. That's because eliminating high-fat items automatically means replacing them with low-fat, low-calorie carbohydrates (fruits and vegetables, breads and grains) and protein (fish, poultry, beans and low-fat milk products).

• Increase exercise. Exercise reduces stress, helps burn more calories and produces a "post-exercise burn"—so that your metabolic rate remains at a higher-than-normal level, even hours after your workout.

Exercise also raises the levels of endorphins, resulting in a nice, drug-free "high." Sustained weight loss is virtually impossible without an ongoing exercise program. If you don't continue to exercise, any weight that is lost will almost certainly return.

Start slowly. Unlike out-of-shape women, out-of-shape men tend to plunge right into a new fitness program, attempting to accomplish too much too soon.

First, get your doctor's OK. Then, begin a brisk-walking program five to six days a week, 20 to 25 minutes a day.

If necessary, break up your exercise into two sessions—morning and afternoon. Increase your time by five minutes per week until you're up to 45 minutes a day. You may want to eventually graduate to slow jogging or a stationary bicycle.

Smart Food Choices

After 15 years of working with both male and female dieters, I've discovered that smart men are nutritionally ignorant—they just don't know what's in the food they're eating and why it can be harmful.

Example: A chef's salad and a diet soft drink is many men's idea of a healthy, low-calorie lunch…but they couldn't be more wrong. A chef's salad is a 750- to 1,000-calorie, high-fat meal, usually containing cheese and luncheon meat (each approximately 100 calories per ounce) and about 80% to 90% fat—all smothered in two or three ladles of dressing (200 to 250 calories).

A man will wash down his chef's salad with a diet drink—and feel virtuous because the soda has no calories. But, in fact, he may have just consumed more than half his caloric and fat limits for the entire day.

Instead of….	Have…
Half a pepperoni pizza	2 regular slices and a green salad
A bran or corn muffin	Bagel or English muffin
A handful of cashews	2 handfuls of popcorn
Chicken nuggets	Broiled chicken sandwich
Fettuccini Alfredo	Pasta with vegetables in tomato sauce
16 ounces of red meat	6 ounces of red meat with a baked potato and tossed green salad

Important: Don't let yourself feel deprived. While you will have to give up the notion that you can eat whatever you want whenever you want it, there is no reason you can't eat the foods you like and still slim down and improve your health. You should try to stick to the rules you have set, but you don't have to be perfect.

Source: Clinical psychologist Morton H. Shaevitz, PhD, director of the behavioral health programs at the Scripps Clinic and Research Foundation in La Jolla, CA. He is the author of *Lean & Mean: The No Hassle, Life-Extending Weight Loss Program for Men.* Berkley Publishing.

CHAPTER ELEVEN

Very, Very Personal

Best Time for Older Men To Have Sex

Older men who have trouble attaining erections at night can do better with morning sex. Testosterone levels are higher earlier in the day.

Source: *Medical Aspects of Human Sexuality.*

Sexual Side Effects of Commonly Prescribed Drugs

In the past, doctors attributed most sexual disorders to psychological causes. But there is a growing awareness—fueled by a growing number of studies—that more than half these conditions are triggered by physical ailments or, more surprisingly, the drugs used to treat these ailments.

Many commonly prescribed drugs produce sexual side effects that most patients—no matter how frightened or delighted they are by the effects—are too embarrassed to discuss with their doctors. Knowing about these drugs ahead of time can help to alleviate the problems.

Drugs that Enhance Sexual Performance and Enjoyment

•*Amphetamines*, once widely used as diet aids, are now used mainly to treat narcolepsy (a condition characterized by uncontrollable attacks of deep sleep) and hyperactivity and attention-span disorders in children. They can cause heightened sexual awareness in both sexes and prolonged erection in males. But, if taken in high doses, they can have the reverse effects—decreased sex drive, inhibited male and female orgasm…and impotence.

•*Amyl nitrate* is a vasodilator (opening up the circulatory blood vessels) prescribed to relieve chest pain brought on by coronary artery spasms. But when crushed under the nose and inhaled (the way it's supposed to be used) just before orgasm, the drug's vapor increases blood flow to the genital area, enhancing and prolonging the feeling of orgasm. In some cases, however, this drug can inhibit orgasm and cause erectile difficulties.

•*Labetalol* is an antihypertensive drug. But unlike most drugs of its kind, which are notorious for causing impotence, this one may actually delay loss of erection after intercourse.

•*Levodopa,* used to treat patients with Parkinson's disease, increases the body's level of dopamine (a natural sexual stimulant) and causes patients to feel sexually aroused. As a result, the drug has been used to treat impotence in otherwise healthy subjects. *Success rate in one study:* 70%.

•*Mazindol*, an appetite-suppressant, can greatly increase female sexual desire.

•*Nitroglycerin* is a vasodilator used to treat patients with angina. It may also increase blood flow to the genitals, thereby facilitating erections in men who have trouble achieving them.

•*Oral contraceptives* can work both positively and negatively. Many women experience a decreased sexual drive when taking the Pill, while others report an increased sex drive. Researchers are still unclear as to why these contradictory effects occur.

•*Papaverine* is another vasodilator which increases the flow of blood to the genitals and is often prescribed to treat impotence. The patient simply injects the drug at the base of his penis immediately prior to intercourse. An erection is almost instantaneous.

•*Phenoxybenzamine* and *phentolamine* are alpha-blockers that are most commonly used to lower blood pressure. But since they prevent the constriction of blood vessels, they are also being used to treat impotence.

•*Valium* and valium-like drugs inhibit sexual performance when taken in high doses. But when given in very low doses to patients with psychologically-caused sexual problems, they enable these patients to relax and become sexually aroused. These drugs can also delay ejaculation and orgasm.

•*Yohimbine* is designed specifically to enhance sexual performance and enjoyment. As a result, it has been touted as the ultimate aphrodisiac. It's especially effective in treating diabetic impotence, which results when the nerves leading to the genital area degenerate.

Drugs that Inhibit Sexual Performance and Enjoyment

•*Alcohol*, ingested alone or in liquid medications (cough medicine, etc.), can cause inhibited erection, decreased sexual desire, delayed ejaculation, male infertility, and gynecomastia (painful breast growth in men).

•*Anabolic steroids* are analogs of testosterone that are prescribed to build muscle tissue in malnourished patients. While they are not widely prescribed, they are widely abused by athletes, especially body-builders. In males these drugs can cause reduced sex drive, impotence, decreased testicle size, and decreased sperm production, gynecomastia, and priapism (prolonged, painful erections). In females, they can cause male-type hair growth and balding, deepening of the voice, reduction in breast size, clitoral enlargement, decreased uterine size, irregular menstruation, and cessation of ovulation.

•*Digoxin* is prescribed to regulate heart beat. It very closely resembles the female hormone estrogen, and can cause decreased sex drive, impotence, and gynecomastia.

•*Estrogen,* used to treat women with certain kinds of cancer and to reduce the unpleasant symptoms of menopause (including vaginal dryness and hot flashes), can cause problems for an older woman's sexual partner. *Reason:* As men age, they may require more and more friction during intercourse to achieve orgasm. But the vaginal lubrication resulting from estrogen supplements decreases this friction.

•*Isotretinoin* (Accutane) is a marvelous drug that has received a lot of attention for its successful treatment of severe cases of acne. It can, however, cause impotence, decreased sex drive, menstrual irregularities, galactorrhea (discharge from the female breasts), and vaginal dryness.

•*Lithium,* prescribed for the treatment of manic depressive disorder, can cause decreased sex drive, inhibited erection, male infertility, and the discharge of milk from female breasts.

•*Nicotine* is a vasoconstrictor that often blocks blood flow to the genitals. As a result, it can cause impotence, vaginal dryness, and even early menopause.

•*Penicillin-derived antibiotics* can accumulate in the semen, triggering allergic reactions in susceptible partners.

•*Thiazide diuretics,* which account for about 90% of diuretics, cause a loss of zinc through the urine. Since zinc is vital to male potency, men using this drug often become impotent.

•*Timolol,* a beta-blocker, is the only eyedrop that has been associated with impotence and decreased sex drive.

Source: M. Laurence Lieberman, a pharmacist in New York and author of *The Sexual Pharmacy.* New American Library. His book lists a total of 226 drugs that are known to influence sexual performance or enjoyment.

Men & Menopause

Not enough men understand what menopause is. As a result, even the most sympathetic man may be thrown completely off balance when the woman in his life begins to exhibit the physiological and emotional symptoms of menopause. Sadly, his ignorance will prevent him from helping the woman he loves...and may even cause him to inadvertently do and say things that make matters worse.

Thanks to books like Gail Sheehy's *The Silent Passage* and Germaine Greer's *The Change,* magazine articles, and TV talk shows, the whole subject of menopause is coming out of the closet. But plenty of myths and misconceptions remain—and they often lead to problems between men—who see in menopause their own mortality—and their menopausal wives. *Answers to basic questions:*

What is menopause? Menopause occurs when the ovaries stop producing the female hormone estrogen and menstruation ceases.

When does menopause typically occur? Menopause is actually a prolonged series of events that occur over years. On average, menopause starts at around age 51, but the symptoms are the most intense during perimenopause—approximately two years before and two years afterward.

What's causing my wife's physical and emotional changes? The hot flashes, the thinning of the vaginal tissues, the decreased vaginal lubrication, the mood swings are all the result of the ovaries producing little or no estrogen now. Any or all of these changes are perfectly normal and to be expected.

Why is my wife less interested in sex now? We've always had a good sex life before. A couple of reasons: The changes in the reproductive tract may make intercourse painful. And hormonal changes may cause a decrease in her sexual desire—even though she probably loves you as much as ever.

Is there any good news? Definitely! Most of the worst symptoms of menopause can be alleviated with hormone-replacement therapy. If she chooses to take hormones, she'll be able to see and feel relief within a matter of weeks. Even if she doesn't take hormones, some of the troublesome symptoms may naturally wane in time. She should discuss her course of action with her gynecologist. *Advantages of hormone therapy:* Control of hot flashes...restoration of integrity of genital tissues...women generally feel better. *Long-term bonus:* Hormonal therapy helps protect against osteoporosis and coronary heart disease. *Disadvantages:* Women with an intact uterus also receive progestin to prevent endometrial cancer, and this can cause resumption of menstruation. *Long-term risk:* Estrogen therapy for more than 15 years can cause a slightly increased risk of breast cancer.

How can I be more supportive of my wife now? Visit the gynecologist with her, so that you can show your support and get your own questions about menopause answered—just as more and more husbands are going to prenatal classes to learn about pregnancy and labor and to be there for their wives.

Give your wife a break. If she's more tired than usual these days, tell her you won't mind if she isn't up to attending the theater or going out after work. *Better:* Make dinner for the two of you, order in…or take her out to eat more often. Don't gripe when she wants to fling open the windows in mid-December—just get yourself another blanket. Offer to rub her feet or bring her a cup of tea. You get the idea.

Anything else? Avoid such inflammatory comments as:

"It's all in your mind!"…"There's nothing wrong with you!"…"You look perfectly fine to me!"

We have to be careful not to make menopause sound like an illness. Without the fear of pregnancy now…with the children perhaps grown and out of the house…with greater time for recreation and for each other, many couples report that this is the happiest time in their life…and that sex is better than ever. Menopause can actually be the start of a wonderful new phase for you both.

Bottom Line

Educated, informed couples are finally starting to treat menopause as the normal, natural life event it is—and less and less as a crisis. Menopause means that a woman is middle-aged, not that it's all over or that she's dying. The current life expectancy for women is 84 years…so there's a lot of life left to be enjoyed—for both of you—after menopause.

Source: Barbara Sherwin, PhD, co-director of the McGill University Menopause Clinic in Montreal and associate professor of psychology and obstetrics and gynecology at McGill University.

Prostate Problems Self-Defense

The good news about prostate cancer is that the disease is almost 100% curable—if it's caught early.

The bad news: Because most men fail to get regular checkups, and because they often ignore the telltale symptoms—chiefly frequent urination, especially at night, and a weak urine stream—most cases of prostate cancer are spotted far too late for successful treatment. *Result:* Prostate cancer now kills more men than all other forms of cancer except lung cancer.

Prostate cancer strikes men of all ages, but it is remarkably common among men in their fifties and sixties. Recent statistics suggest that roughly one of every 20 men age 50 or older has prostate cancer, even though few are aware of the problem. *At special risk:* African-Americans and those with a family history of prostate cancer…

•Having one primary relative (father, brother, or son) with prostate cancer doubles your risk of having the disease.

•Having two increases your risk three to four times.

•Having three raises your risk by a factor of eight to 10.

Recent reports suggesting that having a vasectomy promotes prostate cancer are inconclusive. Men who have had vasectomies do seem to have a higher incidence of prostate cancer. But it's simply not clear yet whether this additional risk stems from the vasectomy itself or merely from the fact that men who get vasectomies tend to see a urologist more frequently than men who do not. In any case, this apparent increase in risk is extremely slight.

Bottom line: Men who have already undergone a vasectomy need not take any special precautions—beyond regular checkups.

To Prevent Prostate Trouble

•Eat less fat. As with heart disease and many other forms of cancer, prostate cancer is more common among men who eat a fatty diet than among those who don't. *Especially dangerous:* Saturated fat, found primarily in meat and dairy products. It seems to be particularly effective at promoting tumor growth. To protect yourself, eat less meat and dairy products. Increase your intake of fruits, vegetables, grains, and non-fat dairy products.

•Don't smoke. Recent studies show clearly that men who smoke face an increased risk of prostate cancer. While this additional risk is small, it's best not to smoke at all—especially if you're elderly, African-American, or if you have a family history of prostate cancer. Try also to avoid exposure to second-hand smoke.

•Have regular checkups. All men should have an annual prostate exam starting at age 50—age 40 for men at risk. This exam should be conducted by a board-certified urologist or radiologist. It should include not only the familiar digital rectal exam, in which the doctor inserts a gloved finger into the rectum to feel for prostate tumors, but also the blood test for prostate specific antigen (PSA). *Cost:* $30 to $75.

An elevated PSA level does not necessarily mean prostate cancer. *Other possibilities:* Enlargement of the prostate (benign prostatic hypertrophy or hyperplasia) or prostate inflammation (prostatitis).

Like prostate cancer, these conditions raise PSA levels. And they cause the same symptoms. Yet unlike prostate cancer, these conditions are generally benign. They can often be controlled with drug therapy.

To pinpoint the cause of an elevated PSA level, the doctor must conduct an ultrasound examination of the prostate. In this procedure, performed without anesthesia on an outpatient basis, the doctor inserts a needle-tipped fiber-optic probe into the rectum.

If any suspicious areas are found, the doctor uses this same probe to take tiny tissue samples. These samples are then biopsied. *Cost:* $300 to $500.

If the biopsy confirms the presence of cancer, your doctor will likely recommend surgical removal of the prostate or radiation therapy. The best treatment for advanced prostate cancer is hormone therapy. Chemotherapy is usually ineffective against prostate cancer.

Source: William J. Catalona, MD, chief of urologic surgery, Washington University Medical Center, St. Louis. He is also urologist-in-chief at Barnes and Allied hospitals in St. Louis. Ninety-five percent of Dr. Catalona's practice is devoted to the treatment of prostate cancer.

Impotence Cure

A device that corrects psychogenic (psychologically-based) impotence is now in clinical trials.

The goal: To free men from lengthy psychoanalysis or the surgery required for implanting a prosthesis.

How it works: A small plastic unit (about 7/8" x 3") is inserted into the rectum, where it is positioned near the nerve center responsible for initiating erections. Next, a tiny transmitter hidden in a piece of jewelry signals the battery-powered insert to generate an electrical field. This prompts a "natural" erection. The device is completely portable, requires no surgery, and can be inserted and removed at will by the user.

Source: Biosonics, Inc., 260 New York Dr., Ste. A, Ft. Washington, PA 19034.

Frequently Misdiagnosed: Vaginal Infections

Most women being treated for chronic yeast infections—either by their internists or by themselves with over-the-counter preparations—actually have a different condition.

Other causes of symptoms: Bacterial vaginosis or herpes infections, which require different treatments than that for yeast infections.

Caution: Never diagnose yourself. Over-the-counter treatments could make your symptoms worse. If you think you have a vaginal infection, ask your doctor to perform a complete physical examination and comprehensive medical history.

Source: Karen Carroll, MD, departments of pathology and infectious diseases, and Paul Summers, MD, department of obstetrics and gynecology, both at the University of Utah Medical Center in Salt Lake City.

CHAPTER TWELVE
Home Smarts

Home Repair Grants

Home owners age 62 and over can qualify for up to $5,000 to repair their homes. *Other requirements:* The home must be in a rural area—population under 10,000...applicants must show that they cannot repay the money.

Source: Farmers Home Administration, Washington, DC or one of their local offices.

Too Many Dangerous Chemicals Are in Too Many of Our Homes

According to the Environmental Protection Agency's estimates, the average household contains between three and 10 gallons of hazardous chemicals—and many of them are organic compounds that vaporize at room temperature.

In the effort to save money by sealing our homes to reduce heating and air-conditioning bills, and by becoming do-it-yourselfers for many tasks once left to professionals, we expose ourselves and our families to high levels of these toxic substances.

Read the Label

"We are all guilty of not thoroughly reading labels," according to Charles Jacobson, compliance officer, US Consumer Products Safety Commission.

If vapors may be harmful, it doesn't do much good to read the label after you have used the product and inhaled the vapors.

Important: Read the labels before buying a product to select the safest in a category. If you find any of the 11 ingredients listed below on a container, avoid buying it. If you must buy it, use extreme caution when working with...

Dangerous Chemicals

1. *Methylene chloride.* A widely used solvent, it is in pesticide aerosols, refrigeration and air-conditioning equipment, cleansing creams, and in paint and varnish removers. Some paint strippers are 80% methylene chloride. Its toxic effects include damage to liver, kidneys, and central nervous system. It increases the carbon monoxide level in the blood, and people with angina (chest pains) are extremely sensi-

tive to the chemical. Methylene chloride has been linked to heart attacks and cancer.

2. *Dichlorvos (DDVP).* Used to control insects. It has a wide range of uses in the home, agriculture and commercial establishments. Currently, dichlorvos is undergoing a special review by the EPA on the grounds that exposure to this compound may pose an unreasonable risk of cancer as well as present other dangers. People may be exposed to dichlorvos by consuming foods with residues of the chemical.

3. *2,4-D.* A weed killer related to Agent Orange—which allegedly caused health problems in exposed Vietnam veterans—2,4-D is widely used by home gardeners and farmers. It does not cause acute toxicity, but its long-term effects are scary—much higher incidence of cancer—and non-Hodgkin's lymphoma has been associated with its use among farmers. The National Cancer Institute also reports that dogs whose owners use 2,4-D on their lawns have an increased rate of a type of cancer closely related to human non-Hodgkin's lymphoma.

4. *Perchlorethylene.* The main solvent employed in the dry-cleaning process, metal degreasing, and in some adhesives, aerosols, paints, and coatings, it can be absorbed through your lungs or your skin. The most common effects of overexposure are irritation of the eyes, nose, throat, or skin. Effects on the nervous system include dizziness, headache, nausea, fatigue, confusion, and loss of balance. At very high exposure it can cause death.

5. *Formaldehyde.* An inexpensive and effective preservative used in more than 3,000 household products. They include disinfectants, cosmetics, fungicides, preservatives, and adhesives. It is also used in pressed-wood products—wall paneling, fiberboard, and furniture, and in some papers. There are serious questions about its safety. It is estimated that 4% to 8% of the population is sensitive to it. Vapors are intensely irritating to mucous membranes and can cause nasal, lung, and eye problems.

6. *Benzene.* Among the top five organic chemicals produced in the United States, this petroleum derivative's use in consumer prod-

ucts has, in recent years, been greatly reduced. However, it is still employed as a solvent for waxes, resins, and oils and is in varnish and lacquer. It is also an "antiknock" additive in gasoline—thus, make sure your house is well ventilated and insulated from vapors that arise from an attached garage.

Benzene is highly flammable, poisonous when ingested, and irritating to mucous membranes. Amounts that are harmful may be absorbed through the skin. *Possible results:* Blood, brain, and nerve damage.

7. *Cyanide.* One of the most rapid poisons known, it is used to kill fungus, insects, and rats. It is in metal polishes (especially silver), in art materials, and photographic solutions.

8. *Naphthalene.* Derived from coal, it is used in solvents, fungicides, in toilet bowl deodorizers, and as a moth repellent. It can be absorbed through the skin and eyes as well as through the lungs. It may damage the eyes, liver, kidneys, skin, red blood cells, and the central nervous system. It has reportedly caused anemia in infants exposed to clothing and blankets stored in naphthalene mothballs. This chemical can cause allergic skin rashes in adults and children.

9. *Paradichlorobenzene (PDB).* Made from chlorine and benzene, it is in metal polishes, moth repellents, general insecticides, germicides, spray deodorants, and fumigants. PDB is also commonly found in room deodorizers. Vapors may cause irritation to the skin, throat, and eyes. Prolonged exposure to high concentrations may cause weakness, dizziness, loss of weight, and liver damage. A well-known animal cancer-causing agent, the chemical can linger in the home for months or even years.

10. *Trichloroethylene (TCE).* A solvent used in waxes, paint thinners, fumigants, metal polishes, shoe polish, and rug cleaners. Tests conducted by the National Cancer Institute showed TCE caused cancer of the liver. A combination of alcohol ingestion with exposure to trichloroethylene can cause flushing of the skin, nausea, and vomiting.

11. *Hydroxides/lye products.* These include automatic dishwasher detergents, toilet-bowl cleaners, fire proofing, paint remover, and drain cleaners. Ingestion causes vomiting, prostration, and collapse. Inhalation causes lung damage. Prolonged contact with dilute solutions can have a destructive effect upon tissue, leading to skin irritations and eruptions.

Source: Ruth Winter, author of *A Consumer's Dictionary of Household, Yard, and Office Chemicals.* Crown Publishers.

When Buying a New Condominium

Buying a condominium is more complicated than buying a house. *Reason:* The purchase is really for two separate pieces of property— your unit and the property held in common. Before signing any contract for a new condominium, which is harder to check out than an established condominium, buyers should study the prospectus for any of these pitfalls:

•The prospectus includes a plan of the unit you are buying, showing rooms of specific dimensions. But the plan omits closet space. *Result:* The living space you are buying is probably smaller than you think.

•The prospectus includes this clause: "The interior design shall be substantially similar." *Result:* The developer can alter both the size and design of your unit.

•The common charges set forth in the prospectus are unrealistically low. Buyers should never rely on a developer's estimate of common charges. *Instead:* They should find out the charges at similarly functioning condominiums.

Common charges include: Electricity for hallways and outside areas, water, cleaning, garbage disposal, insurance for common areas, pool maintenance, groundskeeping, legal and accounting fees, reserves for future repairs.

•*Variation on the common-charge trap:* The developer is paying common charges on unsold units. But these charges are unrealistically low. *Reason:* The developer has either underinsured or underestimated the taxes due, omitted security expenses, or failed to set up a reserve fund.

•The prospectus includes this clause: "The seller will not be obligated to pay monthly charges for unsold units." *Result:* The owners of a partially occupied condominium have to pay for all operating expenses.

•The prospectus warns about the seller's limited liability. But an unsuspecting buyer may still purchase a condominium unit on which back monthly charges are due, or even on which there's a lien for failure to pay back carrying charges.

•The prospectus makes no mention of parking spaces. *Result:* You must lease from the developer.

•The prospectus is imprecise about the total number of units to be built. *Result:* Facilities are inadequate for the number of residents.

•The prospectus includes this clause: "Transfer of ownership (of the common property from the developer to the homeowners' association) will take place 60 days after the last unit is sold." *Trap:* The developer deliberately does not sell one unit, keeps on managing the condominium, and awards sweetheart maintenance and operating contracts to his subcontractors.

•The prospectus specifies that the developer will become the property manager of the functioning condominium. But the language spelling out monthly common charges and management fees is imprecise. *Result:* The owners cannot control monthly charges and fees.

Source: Dorothy Tymon, author, *The Condominium: A Guide for the Alert Buyer.* Golden-Lee Books.

Is Your Property's Assessed Value Too High?

The effective real-estate tax is the tax rate multiplied by the assessed value. There's not much an individual can do about the tax rate, but assessment can often be challenged successfully. *Requirements:* Proof that either the property is overvalued or the assessment is higher than on comparable property in the same area.

When to Ask for a Reduction

•Just before making necessary repairs of damages that have lowered the value.

•Local tax records err in description by overstating size or income.

•Net income drops due to factors beyond owner's control.

•When the price paid for the building in an arm's length transaction is lower than the assessed value.

What to Do

•Determine the ratio of the assessed value to the present market value. Compare against average ratios of similar properties recently sold in the same area. *Sources:* Ratios available to the public in tax districts. Real-estate brokers, professional assessors can also be consulted.

•Check tax records for a description of the property.

•Consult a lawyer on the strength of the case, whether it can be handled by an informal talk with the assessor, and how much it will cost if a formal proceeding and appeal are necessary.

When the New House Is a Lemon

A home buyer may be able to get out of the entire purchase contract if the seller has misrepresented a house with many serious defects.

Normally, when defects show up after the buyers move in, they can sue for damages. Some state courts have ruled that two reasons for suing may void the entire sale: (1) Misrepresentation of an important aspect of the house. (2) The presence of many serious defects.

One case: The builder had assured the buyer that there would be no water problem. But the house was flooded soon after the closing. The court said the related damage would be impossible to repair.

Source: *Chastain v. Billings,* 570 SW2d 866.

How to Sell Your Own Home Fast

When my wife and I wanted to sell our home four years ago, we found that real estate agents weren't for us.

Agents typically charge a commission of around 6%. That means they'll take $9,000 of your equity from the sale of a $150,000 home.

In fact, the biggest myth in real estate is that you need an agent to sell your home.

Selling your house yourself often means selling it faster, and saving thousands of dollars in the process. Since you don't have to inflate your price by the amount of the commission, you'll sell sooner than a comparable agent-listed property.

Almost 60% of all real estate agent listings don't sell during the listing period. Many of these home owners then take matters into their own hands and sell by themselves. *Here's how to sell your own home…*

•Set the right price. Few home sellers know the market value of their property. Get a professional appraisal ($200 to $300). This will tell you the highest possible price to expect for your home in the current market.

Price your home using the appraisal and the market's supply and demand. *Example:* If you're in a tough buyer's market (with many similar homes on the market), price your home at or below appraised value. Our experience shows us that buyers are more likely to make a reasonable offer on a fairly priced home, and no offers on an overpriced one.

•Fix and clean everything. A potential buyer expects a home to be in move-in condition. Buyers will tolerate a little wear and tear, but you're more likely to get a full price offer when the buyer falls in love with your immaculate home.

Pay particular attention to your home's exterior. If the exterior is not in good condition, potential buyers will drive right by without stopping to go inside.

•Use a multipronged approach to advertise your house. A classified ad in the local paper is the traditional route, and sometimes these ads are effective.

But if you want to sell your home fast, yard signs and for-sale-by-owner publications are the way to go.

According to a survey of home buyers by *USA Today*, an astounding 49% of them found their future residence simply by noticing a sign in the front yard.

The most effective way to find buyers is by advertising in magazines that exclusively feature homes for sale by owner. Many regions of the nation now have these widely distributed publications. Also consider making a fact sheet about your house along with a photo.

Internet sites are another new—and inexpensive—way to reach potential buyers. *Our favorite:* www.nfsboa.com, a national network of for-sale-by-owner Web sites.

Source: William Supple, Jr., publisher of *Picket Fence Preview*, for-sale-by-owner real estate magazines serving Vermont, New York and New Hampshire. He is also cofounder of the National For Sale By Owner Association, a nonprofit group that helps home owners sell their own property. Mr. Supple is author of *How to Sell Your Own Home*. Picket Fence Publishing.

When to Watch Your Broker Closely

A company or individual listing property for sale with a real estate agent may find it's no longer listed after an offer is turned down. *Reason:* The agent is trying to make the commission by temporarily taking the property off the active list in the hope the owner will give up and accept the offer. The agent may keep other agents from sending around prospects by removing the file or spreading word that the property has been sold.

Should *You* Refinance Your Home?

Consider refinancing your mortgage if the current rate is at least one percentage point lower than the rate you pay now. For refinancing to make financial sense, you should also intend to live in the house long enough for the savings to wipe out the fees.

Source: Keith Gumbinger, vice president of HSH Associates, a firm that collects interest rate data, 1200 Rte. 23, Butler, NJ 07405.

Keep All Receipts of Home Improvements

Keep *all* receipts related to home improvements—no matter how small. *Sort them into two categories:* Spending to repair or maintain your home—including wallpapering...painting ...patching the roof. Spending to improve your home—including installing energy-efficient windows...building a deck. Keeping good records may help lower your capital gains tax bill should you ever sell the home for gain over the exclusion amount (assuming you qualify for it).

Source: Julian Block, a tax attorney in Larchmont, NY, and a former special agent for the IRS.

CHAPTER THIRTEEN
The Skilled Traveler

How to Travel Free

Instead of traveling cheap, you could be traveling free—from transportation by air—or sea—to lodgings, meals, and entertainment. Most free travel requires no special skills, credentials, or contacts. And it can be just as luxurious—and often more pleasurable—than the most expensive paid vacation.

Cruise lines generally offer a free passage to anyone who recruits 10 to 15 paying passengers. (Many airlines offer similar deals.) If you can't lure that many customers, you can get a pro-rated reduction on your fare.

You can also cruise free as an expert in a pertinent subject. Historians, anthropologists, naturalists, and ornithologists are in especially high demand. Your job on the cruise would be to present a series of lectures and to be available for informal questioning. It helps to have a PhD (or at least a Master's) and to have published articles on the subject, but an affable personality and a willingness to share your knowledge with others can stretch your credentials. After your first cruise in this capacity, a good reference will ease the way at other lines.

Free cruises are available to doctors and nurses who are willing to be on 24-hour call (here a salary is an added inducement)…to athletic directors and coaches who can help organize recreational activities…to musicians and entertainers willing to perform—to cosmetologists who can barter their services for a ride.

There is also a strong demand for "hosts"—distinguished single gentlemen who are usually 55 years old and up. They serve by dining and dancing with the many unattached older women taking these vacation cruises. Besides free room and board, hosts are encouraged to make use of an unlimited bar tab available for themselves and their new female friends.

Source: Robert William Kirk, author of *You Can Travel Free.* Pelican Publishing Co.

Vacation Traps…and Wonderful Alternatives

It's a shame to waste money on a vacation that fails to meet your expectations. *Overrated destinations:*

•*Trap:* Hawaiian "fantasy" resorts. In both architecture and amenities, these multi-million dollar resorts completely lack any feel for the culture of Hawaii. Guest activities include Clydesdale horse riding and gondola sailing on man-made lakes. If fantasy is what you're looking for, go to Disney World instead.

Better: The island of Lanai. Once home to pineapple plantations, the island has recently seen the opening of its first major resorts. *Result:* It still retains the atmosphere of early Hawaii.

•*Trap:* Bermuda in winter. Many vacationers don't realize that this island is located in the Atlantic Ocean, not the Caribbean—at about the same latitude as North Carolina. Winter weather is often rainy and chilly.

Better: Cancun or Cozumel on the Mexican Caribbean. Both offer good winter rates.

•*Trap:* Venice in the summer. Poor sanitation, hordes of tourists, and heat and humidity combine to make Venice smelly and unpleasant in the summer. Visit at another time of year.

Better: If you want both art and canals, try Amsterdam.

•*Trap:* Miami Beach. The city lost its luster long ago. Hotel Row has become crowded and expensive.

Better: Fort Morgan Island on the Alabama Gulf Coast. This 25-mile breaker island is quiet and offers a pleasing southern atmosphere. *Drawback:* Winter weather isn't as mild as in South Florida.

•*Trap:* The overbuilt Caribbean islands. These include Nassau/Paradise Islands in the Bahamas, the Montego Bay area in Jamaica, and the Dutch side of St. Maarten.

Better: The quieter Bahamian islands of Eleuthera and Exuma. If you want quiet and excitement, Anguilla is only a 20-minute ferry ride from the shopping and casinos of St. Maarten.

•*Trap:* All-inclusive resort packages. Offered primarily in the Caribbean and Mexico, these packages include room, meals, and activities all for one price and all under one roof. *Drawbacks:* You pay for amenities (rhumba lessons, for example) that you may not use, and you never experience the surrounding countryside.

Better: Villas, equipped with kitchens and bedrooms, are a better choice. They give you privacy at a good value.

•*Trap:* Traditional cruises. The ships that sail the Caribbean and Alaskan coast make ports of call that, in recent years, have become fake places that are designed to take as much money from tourists as quickly as possible.

Better: Cruise ships and schooners sailing the New England and Canadian coasts or the fjords of Scandinavia offer great cruises. And you don't have to fend off people selling beads every time you step ashore.

•*Trap:* Eastern Europe. Many who travel to the newly free countries of Eastern Europe return home disappointed. *Problem:* They expected to stay in reasonably comfortable hotels and enjoy exciting sightseeing. *Reality:* These countries have neither the hotels nor the tourism infrastructure (guides, buses, etc.) to handle tourists.

Exception: Visit Hungary, where years of goulash capitalism have created a modicum of tourist comforts. Or stay in a bordering country and take day trips to the East. *Bonus:* The Eurail Pass is now good for train travel in Eastern Europe.

•*Trap:* The most popular national parks in summer. Yellowstone and Yosemite are overrun with tourists and tour buses during the summer months.

Better: Visit the undiscovered—but more difficult to get to—jewels of the park system: Glacier in Montana, Boundary Waters Wilderness Area—a canoeist's dream—in Minnesota, and Big Bend in Texas.

•*Trap:* Vermont during the fall foliage season. During a few weeks in autumn, tour buses wend their way through the mountains of Vermont tail-to-trunk like parades of elephants.

Better: Visit the nearby, less crowded, and nearly as breathtaking states of Maine, New Hampshire, and upstate New York.

•*Trap:* Aspen in the winter. Both the prices and the crowds are out of this world.

Better: Visit Aspen in summer when the crowds have abated and the scenery is beautiful in an altogether different way. In winter, try Crested Butte, Colorado. It's less glitzy, a better value, and has equally fine skiing.

Source: An expert who has been writing about travel for more than two decades.

Senior-Citizen Discounts

Offered by most airlines, these discounts are applicable for one companion, regardless of the companion's age—a great travel opportunity for grandparents and grandchildren.

Source: *Bill & Pam Bryan's Off the Beaten Path,* 109 E. Main St., Bozeman, MT 59715.

Fishing a New Lake

If you know where to start looking, you can fish any lake successfully.

Where bass congregate:

•Near trees that have recently fallen into the water.

•*In hot weather:* Under lily pads, especially in the only shallow spots around.

•*In consistently mild weather:* In backwater ponds and coves off the main lake. *Best:* Good weed or brush cover, with a creek running in.

•*Any time at all:* In sunken moss beds near the shore.

Source: *Outdoor Life.*

Hotel-Room-Rate Trap

Paying the rack rate—the price listed in the hotel brochure—for a night's lodging. Call the hotel directly and ask for the best possible rate —weekend packages, seasonal specials, or senior discounts. These will likely be lower than the rate quoted by travel agents and 800-number reservation operators. *Also helpful:* Ask for the corporate rate—available even to individual travelers—which is usually 10% to 15% off the rack rate.

Source: Herb Teison, editor, *Travel Smart,* 40 Beechdale Rd., Dobbs Ferry, NY 10522.

The Best Slot Machines

Vegas rules are most chaotic for slot machines. In Atlantic City, all machines must return at least 83% of the amount wagered...and a few return even more than 83%. But in Nevada, one machine might pay back 99%, while the one right next to it pays back only 60%. The bettor's problem is that it's impossible to identify the hot machines. Their placement is the casino's closely guarded secret.

The best-paying machines are usually found third or fourth from the end of a busy aisle, where the most people will see and hear the payoffs.

Worst payoffs: Any machine near the door of a casino showroom.

Among Atlantic City's casinos, the variations are narrower than in Vegas, but they can still be worked for or against you.

Source: Lee Pantano, Box 47, Atlantic Highlands, NJ 07716.

Bingo Never Was a Game of Chance

Most people play bingo as if it were a game of sheer chance—as if any set of cards had just as good a chance of winning as any other. They are mistaken. If you correctly choose the cards you play, you can significantly improve your odds of winning any bingo game.

The following system works with straight bingo (where you must cover five squares in a row—vertically, horizontally, or diagonally), coverall (a jackpot game, in which you must cover every square on your card), or any other variation.

Key strategy: To get as many of the 75 numbers as possible on a given set of cards. There are 24 numbers printed on every bingo card. (There are 25 squares, but the center square is a non-numbered free space.) If you chose three cards at random, their 72 numbered spaces would represent only 49 different numbers—the other 23 spaces would have duplicate numbers.

It is possible, however, to find sets of three cards with no duplicates—with 72 different numbers. (Time permitting, players can choose their cards freely at the beginning of any session.) If you were to play such a set, you would be 25% more likely to win a given game than a player with a random set. Depending on the size of the prizes, that edge can translate into hundreds—or even thousands—of dollars of winnings within a few weeks.

The Truth About "Lucky" Cards

Ironically, most players choose sets that are worse than random. They look for cards with one or two "lucky" numbers—7 or 11, for example. And they are especially drawn to cards where those lucky numbers are at the corners.

The results are devastating. In an average straight game with 1,000 cards in play, a bingo will occur after 15 numbers are called. That means that any given number—regardless of whether it is "lucky" or not—will be called in only one of five games. In those other four games, any set of cards with an uncalled "lucky" number is 25% less likely to win. (When a number is at a corner, it affects three lines—one vertical, one horizontal, one diagonal.)

Another advantage of choosing non-duplicating cards is that it makes it easier to keep track of the numbers you're covering—and harder to miss one by accident.

There are countless statistical systems favored by bingo players, but this is the only one I've found that generates consistent profits.

Where to Play

The only live variable in bingo is the proportion of money collected that is returned to the players. Most operators hold back at least 50% for overhead and revenue. (The percentage is usually posted on the bingo sheets or somewhere in the hall.)

Other games, however, return as much as 75% to the players. The more money that comes back, of course, the better your chances of coming out ahead.

Source: John "Dee" Wyrick, author of *Complete Authoritative Guide to Bingo.* Gambler's Book Club.

Radio Contests: More Than Luck

Almost every popular radio station uses giveaways. Rewards include cash, cars, vacations, and other prizes, ranging from record albums to TV sets. Playing the contests won't make you rich, but there's nothing like the thrill of hearing your name announced over the radio—as a winner.

Although chance plays the major role, you can greatly increase your odds of winning by understanding how call-in contests are run.

To begin: Pick a few stations that have entertaining contests and good prizes. Listen to each closely for a few hours, and phone in several times to get a feel for how the game is played.

The more contests you enter, the greater your chance of winning. The trick is to do this without spending your life on the phone. *The key:* Each program's disk jockey has a format that he follows closely.

Example: My prime listening time is from 11 pm to 1 am. By monitoring four stations, I have found that one holds regular contests at 42 minutes after the hour, another at either 15 or 45 minutes after the hour, another at either 5 or 35 minutes after the hour, and another at 5 of the hour. I tune into those stations only at those times.

After the contest has been announced, several factors determine how quickly you should place your call:

•The winning number. The number of the winning call often corresponds to the station's location on the dial. For example, one station, at 95.5 FM, always rewards the 95th caller. If you dial right away, you'll be about number 20 (stations generally tell you your number when your call is answered). So wait 35 seconds before dialing. By the time the call goes through and the phone rings a few times (at least five seconds per ring), you'll be pretty close to call number 95. It usually takes the station 70–75 seconds to reach that call.

•The number of lines at the station. This helps determine how quickly they get to the winning number. A station with only two phone lines moves more slowly than one with 22. If you ask, most stations will tell you how many lines they use for contests.

•The number of people answering the phones. Stations that have two or more people handling the calls move more quickly than those where it's left up to the DJ. After you've played the contests a few times, you'll get to know the voices —and the number of phone answerers at each station.

•Individual speeds. Some DJs get the contest rolling quickly; others are slower. Get to know their habits.

There's always an element of chance. The difference between being caller number 94 and caller number 95 is a split second, and there's no way you can control that. But you can greatly increase the odds of winning.

Don't give up. If you get a call through and you're five or more numbers away from winning, hang up and try again. And don't let a busy signal discourage you. *Hint:* Many stations have a recording that says "Please try again later" if all the lines are busy. Stay on the line. Your call will be answered...sometimes in the middle of the recording, sometimes soon after it is completed.

Some DJs award the prize at random rather than counting through the calls to, say, number 95. Others announce that caller number two will win, so they don't have to answer 95 calls (and with such a low number, it's really no contest at all). Your only recourse in such a situation is to complain to the station's management. If lazy DJs know they've been caught, they'll improve.

Source: Bob Gross, who has won more than $10,500 in cash and prizes in radio contests over the past five years.

How to Become a Game-Show Contestant

Getting an audition as a contestant on a game show is easy. But the contestants who make it onto a show—and go on to win—have special qualities. *The edge:* These players know how to put their best face forward, and they know their game.

To Get an Audition

•Target the game show. Your favorite game as a viewer may not be the game you play best.

Important: Choose a vehicle for your best skills and personality traits, matching them to one of the four game-show categories—trivia/quiz, word/puzzle, personality, and kids/teens.

•Prepare diligently. Expertise at a game will compensate for almost any shortcoming. The game-show producers want you to win. Game shows are popular in proportion to the excitement they generate. Winners are exciting.

Key: Watch the game regularly—daily is best. Tape it if necessary. Know all the rules and be familiar with game lingo.

Essential: Practice, practice, practice. *The best ways:* (1) Play along as you watch the game. (2) Play mock games. (3) Play board games, read books and periodicals, and play video/computer/arcade games.

•Get an audition. Some shows pick directly from the studio audience, with little or no preliminary interviewing. *More common:* Watch for a trailer at the end of the show that supplies addresses and/or telephone numbers to contact for audition information. *Best:* Call rather than write. Calling is faster, and you can get immediate answers to your questions.

Smart questions to ask when calling a show: I am planning a trip to Hollywood during the period of _____. When will you be interviewing during that time? Will I have time to get through all my audition interviews during that time? If I qualify, will I be able to tape my shows during that time? Will you be conducting a contestant search in or around my area during the coming months? What is your audition process?

Important: Be polite and to the point in all your conversations.

Source: Greg Muntean, former game-show contestant coordinator for *Jeopardy!* and *Wheel of Fortune.*

Credit-Card Calling

When you have more than one phone call to make from a hotel or pay phone, don't hang up after each call. Push the # button between calls. This will allow you to stay connected with your chosen long-distance carrier. *Added benefit:* Most hotel computers will register several calls made this way as a single local call, saving you surcharges.

Source: *Travel and Leisure,* 1120 Avenue of the Americas, New York 10036.

Choosing the Safest Seats

Myth: That the safest seats on all commercial aircraft are those next to emergency exits.

Reality: Aisle seats close to the overwing emergency exits are safer. These seats are commonly in the mid-front section of the plane. If you sit in the window seat next to an emergency exit, you may be worse off in the event of a crash that jams the exit. Aisle seats near several exits give you more escape options in the event of a crash.

Lifesaving precaution: When you take your seat in the plane, count and memorize the number of rows to the nearest exits. *Reason:* If smoke fills the cabin after a crash, you may have to feel your way in the dark to an exit. This precaution is based on the tactics that crash survivors actually have used to get out of a plane.

Source: Geraldine Frankowski, director, Aviation Consumer Action Project, an advocacy group for airline safety and passenger rights, 2000 P St. NW, Washington, DC 20036.

Airline-Ticket Buying Savvy

When ordering airline tickets, pay for them with credit cards. Along with attractive sale prices as airlines try to lure flyers, the industry is experiencing a spate of bankruptcies. People who pay cash are in danger of losing their money if a carrier goes under. Credit-card customers usually can get a refund.

Source: *New Choices for the Best Years*, 28 W. 23 St., New York 10010.

Combating Air-Travel Fatigue

•*Before takeoff:* Food and beverages. Eat and drink lightly for 24 hours before a flight. *Recommended:* Salads, fish, chicken, wine. *Avoid:* Liquor, bon-voyage parties.

Forty-eight hours before departure: Ask the airline for a special severe hypoglycemia (low blood sugar) in-flight meal. You will probably get a nice seafood salad from the first-class galley, even if you have an economy ticket. On boarding, remind the chief flight attendant about the special meal you ordered.

Clothes: Wear loose-fitting clothing. Bring slip-on shoes. *Reason:* Long hours of sitting can cause swelling of the legs and, especially, of the feet.

Women: If possible, plan a plane trip within 7 to 10 days after the onset of the menstrual cycle.

Medication: Take an adequate supply and a copy of your prescriptions. A note from your doctor can often avoid hassles with overzealous customs officials.

•*In the air:* Avoid consuming all the food and drink offered. Alcohol, nuts, soft drinks, and other foods that have empty calories can cause a swing from high to low blood sugar. You go from feeling great to feeling tired, cramped, and headachy.

Don't do important business work while flying. *Reason:* Decision-making and complicated paperwork add to an already increased stress level. *Better:* Accomplish as much as you can before departure. *Aboard:* Read nondemanding work-related material. *Preferred:* Relax by reading an absorbing book.

•*At your destination:* Changes of time, space, and place can cause a feeling of dislocation. Continue following the airborne guidelines of moderation suggested. Realize that your tolerance level for everything from decision-making to dining are below average while on a short trip abroad.

Source: Warren Levin, MD, and Howard Bezow, MD, World Health Group, 5 World Trade Center, New York 10048.

CHAPTER FOURTEEN

Self-Defense

Police-Impersonator Self-Defense

The color of the flashing lights atop police cars are not standardized across the United States. While red flashers are common, many police forces use combinations on their vehicles, such as blue-and-red and blue-and-white. Other police forces use just blue lights. *Self-defense:* To protect yourself from criminals impersonating highway police—without violating the law—turn on emergency flashers when an unmarked vehicle signals you from behind… stay on the road…slow down …then stop at the first well-lighted, populated area, such as a gas station.

Source: Phil Lynn, manager, National Law Enforcement Policy Center, International Association of Chiefs of Police, Alexandria, VA.

Social Security Ripoff

There are now four million illegal users of fake Social Security numbers. *Result:* Someone else may be receiving your benefits. *Self-defense:* Call the Social Security Administration (800-772-1213) to request your summary statement of earnings. Compare it with your past W-2 statements. Lower annual figures may mean benefits are being misdirected. Higher figures could mean your number has been stolen and could attract the IRS, which scans this data to uncover hidden income. *Statute of limitations for an appeal:* Three years, three months, and three days from the contested year.

Snow-Shoveling Self-Defense

Do not hold your breath and strain when lifting a shovelful—this slows blood flow to the heart. When breath is released, blood pressure suddenly rebounds and becomes significantly elevated—which can create a dangerous heart overload. *Correct way to shovel:* Breathe out as you lift the shovel and toss the snow off to the side.

Source: *Cardiac Alert,* 7811 Montrose Rd., Potomac, MD 20854.

Bathroom Danger

Dirty hotel bathtubs can transmit athlete's foot, skin rashes and other infections. Make sure your tub is dry, smooth and free of cracks. When in doubt, clean it with Comet or a similar product.

Source: Yehudi M. Felman, MD, clinical professor of dermatology, Downstate Medical School, Brooklyn, NY.

How to Protect Yourself From a Package Bomb

Package bombs and letter bombs often have clues to alert recipients to possible trouble. *Danger signs:*

•Excessive weight for the size.

•Too much postage.

•No return address.

•Mailed from a foreign country, or via airmail or special delivery.

•A rigid or lopsided envelope.

•Common words are misspelled.

•Restrictive markings, such as *Confidential* or *Personal.*

•Incorrect title for the addressee, or a title without a person's name.

•Handwritten or poorly typed address.

•Protruding wires or tinfoil.

•Excessive securing material, such as tape or string.

•Oily stains or discoloration on the outside of the package.

If you're suspicious: Don't touch the package—not even to move it out of the way…immediately call your local FBI office, or police or fire department…or call the FBI's Bomb Data Center at 202-FBI-BOMB.

Source: William Carter is with the Federal Bureau of Investigation at their headquarters in Washington, DC.

Age-Discrimination Traps

Age discrimination laws can be circumvented with employment contracts. A federal court recently approved the firing of a man who had an employment contract that expired on his 70th birthday. The man was kept on for six more months, without a contract, then let go. *Court:*

The action did not constitute mandatory retirement, which is illegal, but merely the legal termination of the services of someone whose contract had expired.

Source: *Harrington v. Aetna-Bearing,* USCD No. III, 1/30.

Most Frequent Hospital Bill Mistake

Ninety-seven percent of hospital bills are wrong, and less than 2% of those errors are in the patient's favor. *Average error:* $1,400.

Frequent mistake: Billing for items or services never delivered (lab work, medication, thermometers, wheelchairs, etc.).

Self-defense: Insist on completely itemized bills ...and review them carefully.

Source: Harvey Rosenfield, head of watchdog group Bills Project.

How to Decide Whether to Accept Your Company's Buyout Offer

As more companies resort to cutting their staffs to boost profitability and competitiveness, more and more people are offered early retirement or voluntary separation. When to accept? It depends. *Consider these questions...*

•Where do you stand in your career? If you have reached a plateau...your job is no longer satisfying...or you have been waiting for a chance to start your own company but lacked the necessary capital...a buyout may be ideal.

•How healthy is your company? If you believe the company's problems are temporary—and a smaller staff will create new opportunities for advancement—consider staying. But if you believe that layoffs will follow the offer, it makes sense to accept the offer and leave.

Types of Plans

•Early-retirement plans offer benefits similar to those provided for the company's retirees. Though companies cannot legally target workers by age when offering early retirement, they can structure plans so they are more attractive to people who are nearing retirement. This can be done by adding years to your age and service, which in some cases makes you eligible for greater benefits. By law, though, early-retirement plans are not negotiable.

•Voluntary-separation plans are structured to appeal to workers regardless of age and length of service. In theory these offers are negotiable, but in practice they are usually take-it-or-leave-it deals. Management does not want to offer one employee greater incentives for fear that others will find out and demand identical treatment.

Typical Scenarios

•*Simple case:* The company offers you one month's pay for every year of service. You have been employed for 12 years and therefore get one year's pay. You'll make out well if you find another job in less than a year.

Trap: Medical-insurance costs can reduce a lump-sum buyout significantly. By law, you must be retained in the firm's medical plan for up to 18 months after you leave. But you must pay all costs of the insurance unless the voluntary-separation program provides otherwise.

•*More complex case:* In addition to compensation based on years of service, your company may sweeten the deal by offering to add five years to your age and five years to your length of service. This may make you eligible for benefits you might not otherwise receive.

Opportunity: If you are nearing retirement and are unsure of the company's future, the offer may be perfect.

However, if you intend to find another job and your medical coverage runs out before you're hired, you may be completely uninsurable as an individual in the current marketplace.

Trap: Even if you do find a new job, illnesses covered by your old policy may be excluded by your new one.

Bottom Line

Make medical coverage a priority when deciding whether to accept a buyout deal. If you have any leverage in the negotiation, focus on health benefits rather than on the amount of the lump sum.

Ideally, you want the company to keep paying premiums during the full buyout term. If the company added five years of service to your package, it should consider adding five years of coverage.

At the very least, see if your company will pay for your health insurance during the 18-month period following your departure.

Source: Jim Klein, vice president, Towers Perrin, an international employee-benefits consultant, 245 Park Ave., New York 10167.

CHAPTER FIFTEEN
Retirement Options

How to Find a Good Nursing Home

Most families postpone as long as possible the decision to use a nursing home. Once the decision is reached, the process of selecting a good facility is so painful that often they move too fast. *Good advice:* Give a parent time to get used to the idea. Meanwhile, investigate every possible choice thoroughly.

How to begin: Get lists of accredited homes from your church, fraternal order, state agency on aging, American Association of Homes for the Aging (Suite 770, 1050 17th St. NW, Washington, DC 20036), or American Health Care Association (1200 15th St. NW, Washington, DC 20005).

Evaluating a Nursing Home

1. Accreditation, license, and certification for Medicare and Medicaid should be current and in force.

2. Best to arrive without an appointment. Look at everything. Building and rooms should be clean, attractive, safe, and meet all fire codes. Residents should not be crowded (ask about private rooms; sometimes they're available at reasonable extra cost). Visit dining room at meal-time. Check kitchen, too. Visit activity rooms when in session.

3. Staff should be professionally trained and large enough to provide adequate care for all residents.

4. If the home requires a contract, read it carefully. Show it to your lawyer before signing. Some homes reserve the right to discharge a patient whose condition has deteriorated even if a lump-sum payment was made upon admittance. *Best:* An agreement that allows payment by the month or permits refunds of advance payment if plans change.

5. Find out exactly what services the home provides and which ones cost extra. For example, the expenses of private-duty nurses are not included. Extras, like shampoo and hairset, can be exorbitant. Make a list of the "extras" your parent will need for a comfortable life. Try to supply some of them yourself.

6. Before you decide on a home, you and your parent should talk with the administrator and department heads. Find out who is in charge of what and whom to speak to if problems arise.

Tax note: Complete cost of nursing-home care for the aged is usually deductible as a medical expense.

The Healthiest Places To Retire in the USA

•*Eugene, Oregon:* A university town that's rich in parks and offers myriad fitness activities. A temperate climate allows outdoor exercise year-round.

•*Prescott, Arizona:* With pure air filtered by deep pines, it offers endless fitness activities, a rich cultural life, and adult education at two colleges.

•*Sun Cities, Arizona:* The best controlled-age community (no children allowed), these twin cities are immaculate and safe. Volunteer, cultural, and educational opportunities abound. So do splendid recreational facilities.

•*Kerrville, Texas:* My home, it has pure air and water, lovely hills all around, and fine facilities for exercising body and mind. Living costs are low.

•*Mount Dora, Florida:* A pretty, safe, livable town, it offers excellent biking, hiking, swimming, and more. Nearby Orlando provides rich cultural programs.

•*Durango, Colorado:* Laid-back and surrounded by spectacular mountains, it has a strong fitness orientation. Its people are energetic, up-beat, and well-educated.

•*Boulder City, Nevada:* This safe, casual town offers fitness activities such as hiking, swimming, tennis, and canoeing. *For rich culture:* Las Vegas is nearby.

•*Bradenton, Florida:* Near glamorous Sarasota, with its rich cultural and educational life, lies more affordable Bradenton, offering outdoor walking, swimming, tennis, and fitness classes, among other pursuits.

Source: Norman D. Ford, author of *The 50 Healthiest Places to Live and Retire in the United States.* Ballantine Books. Ford has been living the low-risk lifestyle for more than 30 years without a day of illness.

Businesses You Can Start for Under $500

Starting a business is not as hard as you think. You don't even need a great deal of money to launch one. Here are several businesses that you can run out of your home with an investment of $500 or less…

•Credit-repair service. Customers usually seek this service after being rejected for a home or car loan. You would resolve their credit disputes, set up payment schedules with credit-card companies, etc.

Key: Screen potential clients. You want those you can actually help. To be eligible for your services, problem accounts must have been paid off for at least one year, preferably three or four. Guarantee clients an overall improvement in their credit.

Cost: $500 for office expenses, placement of ads in area newspapers, research of credit recordkeeping and reporting laws. *Earning potential:* $100,000 a year.

•Estate sales. Visit estate sales and study the business before soliciting clients of your own. You will need to learn how to price antiques and how to draw up a contract with clients.

Key: Letting clients know that you will take care of everything.

Cost: $200 to $300 to advertise your service in daily and shoppers' newspapers. The clients pay to advertise sales. *Earning potential:* 25% of sales.

•Meeting planner. Put together events, meetings, and conventions for clients.

Key: Pay attention to details. Thoroughly research hotels, restaurants, meeting facilities, and travel arrangements you make for clients. Your business will grow through word-of-mouth referrals.

Cost: $500 for office expenses, yellow pages ad. *Earning potential:* $30,000+ a year.

Source: Stephen Wagner, associate publisher and editor of *Income Opportunities* magazine and author of *Mind Your Own Business: The Best Businesses You Can Start Today for Under $500.* Bob Adams, Inc.

How to Make Money As a Consultant

At one time or another, most executives consider selling their expertise on their own, as consultants. The majority are at least moderately successful, but many fail. Most commonly, they overestimate the salability of their services and underestimate the effort needed to sell them.

Pitfalls for New Consultants

•Not realizing that consultants, especially new ones, spend more time selling their services than performing them.

•Wasting time on unproductive prospects.

•Choosing too broad a field in which to consult.

•Not learning to talk the client's language. This is essential because many consultants sell a highly specialized service with its own vocabulary to an equally specialized customer who uses a completely different language. *Example:* A computer expert who is hired to automate market research for a diaper manufacturer.

To sell their services, successful consultants:

•Maintain pressure by keeping in touch with clients and prospects.

•Master such sales and marketing methods as the art of writing letters, making convincing phone calls, and developing presentations.

•Start at the top, contacting the chief executives of the Fortune 1000 companies.

Source: Charles Moldenhauer, VP, Lefkowith, Inc., marketing and corporate-communications consultants, New York.

Working After Retirement

Many retirees would like to keep working after retirement, at least part-time. But those who want to work for financial reasons should be aware of these drawbacks:

•You can work and still collect Social Security benefits, but for every $2 earned above a government-determined ceiling you lose $1 in benefits if you are under age 65. When you add your commuting costs, job-related expenses, and payroll deductions, you may find part-time work doesn't pay off.

•If you continue working part-time for the same company, you may not be eligible to collect your pension. One way around this, if the company will go along, is to retire as an employee and return as a consultant or freelancer. Since you're now self-employed, your pension won't be affected.

A very attractive alternative to working part-time is to start your own business. Professionals such as lawyers can often set up a practice, setting their own hours. Or you might turn a hobby into a business.

Source: William W. Parrott, a chartered financial consultant at Merrill Lynch, Pierce, Fenner & Smith, Inc., 1185 Avenue of the Americas, New York 10036.